GW00390952

WILLIAM CAREY
Pioneer Missionary

WILLIAM CAREY
Pioneer Missionary

E. A. Annett

AMBASSADOR
Belfast Northern Ireland **Greenville** South Carolina

William Carey - Pioneer Missionary
This edition 2000

All rights reserved

ISBN 1 84030 075 2

Ambassador Publications
a division of
Ambassador Productions
Providence House
Ardenlee Street,
Belfast, BT6 8QJ
Northern Ireland
www.ambassador-productions.com

Emerald House
427 Wade Hampton Blvd.
Greenville,
South Carolina 29609, USA
www.emeraldhouse.com

CONTENTS

LIST OF ILLUSTRATIONS

WILLIAM CAREY

——◆——

CHAPTER I.

THE BOY.

"Boyhood history is carved deep."

PLAIN and unromantic was the greater part of
Northamptonshire, and more especially the
district of Kettering, in the eighteenth century. Here
villages and towns lay close together, inhabited by
folk whose lives were as grey and dull as the stone,
dark-thatched houses in which they lived. Boot-
makers, weavers, and agricultural labourers, poorly
paid and ill-nourished, they eked out a scanty liveli-
hood which was really one long, grim struggle with
poverty.

In such a neighbourhood stood the village of
Paulersbury, in which, on the 17th of August 1761,
William Carey was born.

He was the eldest of a family of five, and his father,
Edmund Carey, was a weaver. When William was
scarcely six, however, Carey the weaver succeeded to
the post of parish clerk and village schoolmaster, and
the family removed to the cottage adjoining the tiny
schoolhouse.

Primitive indeed was the school, with its benches

roughly made of small trees, sawn down the middle, and standing on legs equally unpretentious. But the cottage was the brightest spot in the village, for not only was it guarded in front by the playground with its wide-spreading plane trees, but at the back was an orchard and garden. Stretching away from its very wall ran the royal forest of Whittlebury, the home of birds and flowers and peacefulness. Out from the school gate, down by the forest edge, was a land of delight for the boys, where flowers blossomed and birds nested and endless opportunities offered for exploration; and the purling brook that trickled through the village supplied further interests. Near the church was the village green, the place for lusty sport, with a deep draw-well in the middle which yielded the sweet refreshment of crystal clear water, cool in the hottest summer day.

A boy among boys was William Carey, wiry and nimble, active in every sport, and possessed of a dogged perseverance that ranked him high in his schoolfellows' estimation. Gentle though he was in disposition, there dwelt within him a spirit that brooked no defeat. Once, it was afterwards remembered, when endeavouring to secure a nest that had baffled his companions, he fell and was carried home bruised and stunned. But as soon as he was able to leave the house the first thing he did was to try again, and his attempt ended in a triumph of achievement.

No tree was too high or too difficult for him. It was commonly known even in those days that whatever he began he finished. Difficulties never seemed to discourage him. Rustic in dress and manners like all his companions, there was yet something in the lad that impressed those he met, and from the quiet face there looked eyes that with their steady, unfearing gaze were an index to the boy's soul.

His education in the schoolhouse was scanty, but an insatiable desire for knowledge possessed him. The entire neighbourhood was laid under contribution for his reading, but he had to be content with a small selection in a rural district where the average wage was little more than five shillings a week. Books of a scientific or historical character were read with avidity, but "novels disgusted me," he wrote in a retrospect, "and I avoided them as I did books of religion, and perhaps from the same motive. I was pleased with romances, and this circumstance made me read the *Pilgrim's Progress* with eagerness, though to no purpose."

With a boy's relish he gloried in travel or adventures. Captain Cook was then the hero of the day, and he returned from his second voyage while Carey was still at school. England was greatly stirred by the story of these voyages, and Carey read the narrative with an admiration that coloured all his after thinking. Among his playmates his nickname was Columbus, and he made such an impression upon them that they would call on him to preach, which he readily would do from an old dwarf witch elm. It was about seven feet in height, and provided not only a pulpit for the preacher, but seats for his enraptured audience. His preaching, however, could scarcely have been religious, and perhaps the most popular theme was Cook in the islands of the Southern Seas.

But it was to Nature that most of all he turned in his quest for knowledge. To a clear and vigorous intellect he added unusual powers of observation, which were combined with a splendid memory. It is said he was lacking in imagination, but his unre-

mitting industry supplied its place, and the natural
world about him became as an open book. Birds,
beasts, insects, flowers, all were sources of unfailing
pleasure to him. His own little room, a luxury un-
dreamt of by most of his companions, became a museum.
Insects were stuck in each corner, living plants and
birds were on every hand, so that he might watch their
development.

"Though I often used to kill his birds by kindness,"
his sister wrote in a charming description, "yet when
he saw my grief for it, he always indulged me with the
pleasure of serving them again, and often took me over
the dirtiest roads to get at a plant or an insect. He
never walked out, I think, when quite a boy without
observation on the hedges as he passed, and when he
took up a plant of any kind he always observed it
with care. . . . He always seemed in earnest in his
recreation as well as in school." These glimpses of his
early days aptly foreshadow the man.

His uncle was a gardener in the same village, and gave
him his first lessons in horticulture. The lad soon
became responsible for his father's garden, and in his
care it was the best-kept in the neighbourhood. If
there was an unproductive spot he planted a tree or
shrub in it; and he found room for a variety of choice
flowers, which he collected with difficulty and tended
with the utmost solicitude. From that time onward
his love for botany never waned until he created at
Serampore the botanical garden which was for many
years the finest in Southern Asia.

During his earliest years his grandmother had lived
with them up to the time of her death, and she had
made him her especial care. She was a woman of
delicate nature and devout habits, and we may be sure

her influence was deep though for the present unnoticed. She was the only real minister of religion he had during boyhood. His father was a man of strict integrity, but lacking in evangelical light and fervour, and his training, though direct, was scarcely calculated to appeal to a boy of Carey's type. The Church services did little more for him than for the majority of those who attended them. Although, as we have seen, he eschewed religious books, his reading was some help to him, for "from my infancy," he wrote, "I had been accustomed to read the Scriptures, and I had a considerable acquaintance with them, especially with the historical parts."

And so he grew to youth with an education received from parents, Nature, and books which, with his habits of observation and perseverance, made him better instructed than most boys of even a better class in those days. But before him there was nothing to rouse hopefulness and expectation. He seemed destined to join his playmates in the field as an obscure agricultural labourer earning five shillings a week, with the poorhouse in sickness or old age.

At twelve years old it was to this work he went, and from it he was only saved by a disease which affected his face and hands most painfully whenever long exposed to the sun. His attempts at work were followed during two tedious years by distressing agony at night; and so at the age of fourteen he was apprenticed to a shoemaker in the neighbouring village of Hackleton.

This was all in the good providence of God, whose guiding hand is to be seen throughout Carey's life, for his new occupation, because of its mechanical character, was one which gave him abundant opportunity for thought.

CHAPTER II.

THE COBBLER.

"The exciting thing about these years of budding emotion is that peril and possibility are both at their highest pitch."

BASIL MATTHEWS.

THE late Professor James in one of his last writings suggested that in preference to the conscription advocated by the militarists, everyone on entering manhood should share in the hard work of the world. This is the experience of very many without any planning beforehand, and so it certainly was with Carey. From the day when he started his new trade to the day when he was laid to rest in distant Serampore, his share in the "work of the world" was never light.

His long hours of labour in the shop at Hackleton were passed in the company of men whose conduct was gross, and it was not long before he followed them in their habits. "Lying, swearing, and other sins," he sorrowfully records, and there was every danger of his sinking to the depths of the ordinary villagers of his time.

His master died at the end of Carey's second year of apprenticeship, and he transferred his services to a Mr. Old, another of the same craft in the village. The senior apprentice at the new workshop happened to be a dissenter and a lad of earnest purpose, whose influence over Carey was destined to be great. But it was not so in the beginning. As son of the parish clerk, Carey had imbibed a deep contempt for dissenters, and, backed up by his new master, a strict churchman, though of rather loose habits, he maintained long and fierce arguments with his workmate.

"I had a share of pride," he afterwards acknowledged, "sufficient for a thousand times my knowledge; I therefore always scorned to have the worst of an argument, and the last word was assuredly mine. I also made up in positive assertion what was wanting in argument, and generally came off in triumph. But I was often convinced afterwards that although I had the last word my antagonist had the better of the argument, and on that account felt a growing uneasiness and stings of conscience gradually increasing."

The habit of careful observation that Carey had already acquired and his natural bias towards fairness and truth came to his assistance, and the consistent life of the older apprentice had its reward. Carey gradually yielded to the importunities of the other, and left off the grosser sins into which he had fallen, and even became willing to accompany him to the chapel, to a weekly prayer-meeting. The new associations awakened longings in his breast, and the desire for godliness became before long a controlling passion. He attended church thrice on a Sunday, became regular at the dissenting prayer-meeting, and sought opportunities for private prayer and heart-searching.

Peace did not come quickly nor easily to the burdened lad. Though his conduct was so much improved as to cause comment in his own home, it was only after two years of secret conflict that he fought his way through to the light. The dawn did not come for him in a burst of glory; it was rather like one of our wintry days when clouds hang heavily over the horizon and we are only sure that the sun has risen by the steady light about our path. After bitter disappointments over his inability to run the straight race in his own strength, and with a deepening conviction that he was ruined and helpless, he tells us that it was through a tract of Robert Hall's that he came to see the crucified Christ as his Saviour. The sun was up long before he was aware of it; but once he knew it was risen, it was never again obscured for him.

No sooner were his own feet upon the rock than, with characteristic energy, he threw himself heartily into the work of rescuing his fellows. He had gradually drifted from the Church of England, and now found a spiritual home among the Baptists, of whom there were many congregations in that district. In Hackleton and the surrounding villages, and even in his own home, he began to preach with much acceptance. His controversial spirit died away with his youthful conceit, and the resentment even of his stern father broke down before the humble earnestness of the young man.

Never did a budding preacher apply himself more conscientiously to his new labours. Within a short time he had made sufficient progress in languages to be able to study the portion he preached upon in Greek, Latin, and Hebrew; and yet the congregations of village dissenters to whom he ministered were illiterate and unable to appreciate his learning. The cobbler's shop was his college, and the only human assistance he received was from those ministers in the neighbourhood who could spare him a little of their time.

Before he was twenty years of age his employer died, and he took over the small business, and about the same time married Dorothy Plackett, the sister of his employer's widow. Both of these steps were mistakes. His wife, though a good woman, was illiterate, and a predisposition to mental disease was against her from the beginning. She had no sympathy with him in his undertakings, but never during the twenty-five years of their married life did he fail to show her the utmost reverence and kindness. The tenderness of his conduct toward her places the nobleness of his character in strong relief.

Not long after his marriage he had to sell off his stock at a loss owing to a depression in trade. Sickness invaded his home and carried off his infant child. He himself was attacked with the fever and ague for which the district was noted; this rendered him prematurely bald and left him in such feeble health that for more than a year he was unfit for work. They were in the greatest straits for food.

By the help of friends and with a small collection raised for him in Paulersbury, he was enabled to remove to an adjacent hamlet, where he taught in the village school to eke out the slender income he obtained from his shoemaking. Teaching was most distasteful to him, however, and he was a signal failure at it. "When I kept school," he naïvely admitted, "the boys kept me." His lot was indeed a hard one, but he never ceased to do all that was in him to spread the gospel—the work to which he felt himself called.

Let us pause here to notice the remarkable association into which Carey had come by his residence at Hackleton. The neighbouring town of Olney contained neither a wealthy nor a wise community, and yet in it and near it there dwelt at this time a galaxy of choice spirits. Cowper the poet was living there, and his pastors in the parish church were John Newton, the great preacher, and after him Thomas Scott, the re-nowned commentator. Sutcliff was the Baptist pastor, while in neighbouring churches Ryland and Fuller were ministering.

To all of these ministers Carey owed a great debt. Scott had marked him out as a young man of promise when he had first seen him as an apprentice at Mr. Old's, and henceforward became his adviser and warm friend. Fuller, too, by his kindly counsel and en-couragement was a ministrant of God to the immature preacher of Hackleton. It was Sutcliff who set apart one evening a month for an interdenominational prayer-meeting for the spread of the gospel, and who re-published a work on prayer and evangelism by Jonathan Edwards. That prayer-meeting and that pamphlet supplied the atmosphere in which before long the first Missionary Society was born. Nowhere in England, in all probability, could there have been found a more favourable spot for Carey's peculiar character and mission; and it is to the everlasting honour of the toiling and careworn district of Olney that here was created by God a cradle for the mighty enterprise of foreign missions.

In 1783, at the age of twenty-two, Carey was baptized by Dr. Ryland the elder, in the river Nen, and joined Mr. Sutcliff's church in membership. Two years later, when the question of Carey's call to the ministry came before that church, the members expressed a doubt whether he possessed sufficient ability to make a useful minister, and the point was carried chiefly through the personal influence of the pastor. With an almost prophetic instinct, this call was detailed as " to preach the gospel wherever God in His providence might call him." He had been preaching for some two or three years past at the village of Earl's Barton, where the congregation looked upon him as their pastor while still formally unordained, and paid him a small allow-

THE COBBLER'S SHED AT HACKLETON TO-DAY.

ance—so small, however, as to be "not sufficient to pay for the clothes worn out in their service."

In 1786 he removed to Moulton, where he was formally invited to become pastor of the dissenting church at a salary of £16 a year in all. He was attracted there by the prospect of a school, from which he hoped for a sufficient increase to his income to enable him to live in some comfort, and to leave for ever his shoemaking, a trade distasteful to him from its utter absence of outlook. In this he was mistaken, for the school never prospered : he failed to exercise any control over the pupils, who took personal liberties with him that subverted all discipline. He was forced to betake himself again to his cobbling, and once a fortnight he might be seen trudging wearily the eight or ten miles to Northampton with his pack full of shoes for sale. The family was miserably poor. On one occasion, when attending the local association meetings in a distant town, he had no money for food, and when the others adjourned for dinner he went for a sharp walk to disguise from them the fact that he was hungry.

His character was rapidly developing, and he was already a man of firm, unshaken faith and determination. Through poverty and unremitting toil he continued his threefold labour of preaching, shoemaking, and teaching. The story is told that on one occasion he was remonstrated with for the length of time he gave to the ministry, which, it was remarked, was seriously hindering his business. " My business," he said proudly, " is to preach the gospel; I only cobble shoes to pay expenses."

Residence at Moulton, despite his pecuniary difficulties, was made agreeable by the wider opportunities he had for mental cultivation. Here he engaged in regular Bible study and commenced that systematic economising of time which he adhered to through life, and which enabled him to accomplish labours that seem incredible. There were many conversions attending his preaching here, and the small chapel proved so inadequate that an extension of premises became necessary.

His last home charge was Leicester, to which town he went in 1789 to a sorely divided church. Poverty still attended him, and he continued to work in his leather apron; but his greatest difficulties arose from the spiritual condition of his congregation. A school conducted here answered better than those in previous places, and he enjoyed the society of a group of cultured and literary men.

Fuller thus wrote of the ministry at Leicester: "His zeal and unremitting labour in preaching the word, not only in Leicester, but in the villages near it, endeared him to the friends of religion, and his thirst for learning rendered him respected by others. The natural energies of his mind, accompanied as they were with a generous, manly, and open disposition, together with an ingratiating behaviour toward men of every degree, soon rendered him respected, not only by those who attended his ministry, but by many other persons of learning and opulence."

Ministers even from London took note of him, and it was apparent that a career of wide usefulness and honour was opening rapidly before him.

CHAPTER III.

THE VISION.

"Whoso hath felt the spirit of the Highes
Cannot confound nor doubt Him nor deny:
Yea, with one voice, O World, tho' thou deniest,
Stand thou on that side, for on this am I."
F. W. H. MYERS.

"WHAT good is it doing your boys?" was the
question asked of a Sunday-school teacher who
had attempted week-evening gatherings with his
scholars. "I'm not sure that it's doing them much
good," he replied ruefully, "but it's doing me a lot."
And it may be that the school at Moulton was not
very successful from the boys' standpoint, but to Carey
it was hallowed as the place where a revelation came
to him from God.

Geography was his favourite subject for teaching,
and it was while he taught his class from a leather
globe of his own construction that it flashed painfully
across his mind how large a portion of the world's
inhabitants were in the darkness of heathendom.
The idea grew upon him until it haunted him by day
and by night. In his workshop he had upon the wall
a huge map, made of many pieces of paper pasted
together, on which he entered all the information he
could gather regarding the population, religion, government, and customs of each country. His mind was

appalled at the awful need, and his spirit became heavily burdened. All his early love for travel, his largely increased knowledge of the earth and of the condition of Christian work, his study of Scripture, and his devotion to Christ were now focused into a fierce energy of love for the heathen.

In him there was nothing of that indolence which contents itself with dreams rather than with deeds. At a meeting of ministers held soon after his ordination he suggested as a subject for their discussion, " The duty of Christian people to spread the gospel among the heathen." He had already urged this in private among his brethren, but none were prepared for such an outburst of zeal. Even his greatest friend, Fuller, startled by the magnitude of the idea, was too amazed to speak. The elder Ryland, who had baptized him a few years earlier, rose sternly to his feet with the rebuke, " Young man, sit down ! When God pleases to convert the heathen, He will do it without your aid or mine ! "

Nothing daunted, he returned to his home and set himself to write a pamphlet which should embody his convictions, and entitled it, " An Enquiry into the Obligation of Christians to use Means for the Conversion of the Heathen." It was as remarkable for its cultured and finished style as for the wide knowledge it showed of the statistics and geography of the world. Race after race, country after country was surveyed, the results being tabulated with a logical exactness that compels admiration. Few men in England of that day, even with the advantages of a University training, could have produced what this obscure toiler of less than thirty years of age compiled in his tiny workshop. It was the first great missionary treatise in the English language, and it has seldom if ever been surpassed.

It reveals, too, the man himself; for while he was writing it, his family and he were in a state bordering on starvation. For weeks they had been without meat and with but a scanty supply of bread. The hunger of his body was forgotten in the greater hunger of his soul for the unhappy millions who sat in darkness and in the shadow of death.

Meanwhile, no stone was left unturned to influence his fellow-ministers. Fuller says: "He would also be frequently conversing with his brethren on the practicability and importance of a mission to the heathen, and of his willingness to engage in it. Some of our most aged and respectable ministers thought . . . that it was a wild and impracticable scheme that he had got into his mind, and therefore gave him no encouragement. Yet he would not give it up, but would converse with us, one by one, till he had made some impression on us." His sister adds her testimony: "He was always, from the first, remarkably impressed about heathen lands. . . . I never remember his engaging in prayer, in his family or in public, without prayer for those poor creatures."

With dogged pertinacity, undismayed by rebuffs, for four years he laid the matter on the hearts and consciences of his fellows. "Now in a greater degree than ever before, his indomitable energy was called into play; difficulties seemed only to spur him on, and he carried all before him. Neither poverty nor disease, neither the discouraging remarks of his friends nor the unsympathetic conduct of his wife, had any effect on his tenacity of purpose—or, if effective at all, they only strengthened it." In 1791 he urged the responsibility of the Church with such vigour that it was allowed that something should be done. But even his warmest friends shrank back from pledging themselves to any undertaking. To save time, they advised him to revise his Enquiry and have it published.

At the next Association meeting held at Nottingham in 1792, Carey was privileged to be the preacher for the occasion. Here he delivered his great sermon from the text in Isaiah liv. 2, 3: "Enlarge the place of thy tent, and let them stretch forth the curtains of thy habitations; spare not, lengthen thy cords, and strengthen thy stakes; for thou shalt break forth on the right hand and on the left; and thy seed shall inherit the Gentiles, and make the desolate cities to be inhabited."

He proceeded to draw two great principles from the text, in the now historic words, "EXPECT GREAT THINGS FROM GOD; ATTEMPT GREAT THINGS FOR GOD." The accumulated energy and zeal that had been gathering ever since his early perusal of Cook's *Voyages* was poured with irresistible power into his theme. He pleaded the cause of the heathen world with agonising earnestness, and denounced the indifference of the Church so powerfully that all were deeply affected. Even Dr. Ryland himself acknowledged that he should not have been surprised if the audience had lifted up their voice and wept.

It was a moment of supreme victory for the young enthusiast; and yet it failed to remove the hesitation felt by many. Seeing they were about to depart, Carey seized Fuller's hand and wrung it in his distress, demanding whether they were going to separate without doing anything. The expostulation was successful, and before the assembly broke up a resolution was recorded that a plan should be prepared against the next meeting for the establishment of a Society for the Propagation of the Gospel abroad.

It was in the October of that same year the meeting was held at Kettering. In the evening a body of thirteen men met in Widow Wallis's back parlour. Fuller says: "There was little or no respectability among us, not so much as a squire to sit in the chair or an orator to address us with speeches." The enthusiasm of the last meeting appears to have somewhat cooled down, but all objections were again overruled by Carey's ardour, and under the irresistible influence of his mind the Baptist Missionary Society was formed, "to carry the gospel to some portion of the heathen world."

Had these men foreseen that their obscure effort was to be followed by the uprising of all modern missionary enterprise, they might have lost themselves in joy. But theirs was a step in the dark. Long they deliberated, and the result was the appointment of a committee to take definite action. A subscription was called for, and these thirteen men who had seen the vision gave the first collection. It amounted to £13, 2s. 6d., and was *all in gold.* Those were the days of guineas; twelve of the men gave a guinea each, and one gave half a guinea. To crown it all, Carey rose to his feet, and formally offered himself for the work, declaring his readiness to embark at once for any part of the world that they might decide upon.

CHAPTER IV.

THE VENTURE.

" His word was in my heart as a burning fire shut up in my bones, and I was weary with forbearing, and I could not stay."—JER. xx. 9.

INTEREST in the missionary scheme spread over the Midlands, and money came in to the Committee beyond all their expectations. Their hopes could not have been very large, however, for some months later they still had received considerably less than £200 for the mission treasury.

The gifts were largely those of the poor, such as the schoolmaster at Olney, who, greatly stirred at a meeting addressed by Carey, records in his diary giving sixpence to the collection. The ministers of the larger centres, especially of London, held rigidly aloof from the movement, prejudiced apparently by its obscure origin. Some cavilled at the idea of a village cobbler going forth on such an errand, surely forgetting that the Master Himself had been sneered at with the words, "Is not this the carpenter?"

The formation of the Society was but the beginning of difficulties. Carey himself had to face the most serious in the opposition of his family. His father said on hearing of it, "Is William mad?" and his wife bluntly refused to go. Timid by nature, failing to appreciate her husband's object, the undertaking meant to her nothing less than ruin. "Perplexed, but not in despair," Carey felt he could not draw back without guilt on his soul; and it was proposed that he should take with him his eldest son, Felix, the rest of the family joining him when he had a home ready for them.

The question of the field to be entered arose next. The world was before them; no doors were specially open, none were known to be shut. Carey mentioned Africa, but he was most keen on going to Hawaii, where Captain Cook had been slain by the fickle island-ers. Another suggested the Pelew islands because of an account he had recently read of a shipwreck there! But He that sitteth in the heavens had His plans, and these proposals did not commend themselves to the group of earnest men who had sought His guidance.

His will was shown in a remarkable manner. A surgeon named Thomas, a godly man but most erratic, had attempted missionary labours in Bengal, assisted by some Christian officials of the East India Company. His capriciousness, extravagance of views, and an unfortunate habit of running into debt, had disgusted his friends, and now he had come to England to seek assistance in founding a mission to the Bengalis. Hearing of Carey, he wrote fully to him of his desire, and this letter was laid before the Committee, who at once determined to see whether they could unite with Thomas in the Bengal Mission.

Scarcely had they arrived at this decision when the door opened and Thomas himself entered. This unexpected and dramatic event awakened Carey's deepest feelings, and springing to his feet to meet him, "they fell on each other's necks and wept."

With an ingenuousness characteristic of the man, Thomas told them of his pecuniary embarrassments,

that he was hopelessly in debt; but his frankness and
zeal won the confidence of the Committee, and it was
immediately decided that Carey and Thomas should go
together in the spring to India. Carey in his enthusiasm
spoke of India as a gold mine, into which he was willing
to descend if the men at home would hold the ropes.[1]
This they heartily undertook to do.

But obstacles still continued to multiply in the path,
and well was it for the new mission that the Committee
was formed of resolute men who, having put their hand
to the plough, despised the thought of looking back.
First of all, their funds were painfully inadequate for
the undertaking; indeed, they had not enough even for
the voyage. This necessitated a preaching tour for the
raising of further money, during the course of which
Carey met Ward, the editor and printer, at Hull, and
with prophetic insight said, "We shall want a man of
your business to print the Scriptures; I hope you will
come," which he did, five years later.

It was decided in committee that to float the new
enterprise, "£100 or £150 a year would be needed
between them all"—that is, for two missionaries, their
wives, and four children—"until they should be able to
support themselves like the Moravians." As a matter
of fact, they received a total of just £200 for the first
three years, apart from the expenses of the voyage.

The money for the journey secured, the next difficulty
that confronted them was how should they reach their
destination? The whole of Indian trade was the
monopoly of the East India Company, and they
jealously guarded against the introduction into India

---

[1] It has recently been asserted that Carey never used the well-
known words, but that Fuller, in recording the meeting, wrote that
"Carey, as it were, said . . ."—E. A. A.

of persons other than those who held a licence from themselves. Inquiries regarding such a licence revealed the utter unlikelihood of it being granted, because of the strong prejudice at the India House against the evangelisation of the natives. The despotic directors of the Company cared not a whit for the moral advancement of the country, and were fully determined not to admit any whose influence might in the slightest degree jeopardise their enormous gains. Even to apply for a licence seemed unwise, for it would bring the venture under the direct notice of the bureaucrats. It was therefore decided that the missionaries should proceed without leave, and take all risks.

A passage was taken in the *Earl of Oxford* Indiaman, a vessel in which Thomas had once been employed as a surgeon; and Carey with his son and his associate repaired to the Isle of Wight, and from there joined the vessel. Two months were spent in idleness while the ship lay at anchor in the Solent, waiting a convoy, for the Channel swarmed with privateers. This delay was a peculiar trial to Carey, for during the whole time Thomas was engaged in various devices to elude his creditors, who relentlessly pursued him. Carey's honourable feelings were deeply wounded by the disreputable position of his friend, yet he did not feel free to draw back.

At length the fleet appeared, and preparations were made for sailing. It was at this inauspicious moment that the captain of the *Oxford* received an anonymous letter, apparently from one of Thomas's disappointed creditors, intimating that information would be lodged against him for having on board an unlicensed person. Immediately the party were put on shore, and only part of their passage money was returned to them.

In deep affliction, but not despondent, Carey wrote to Fuller, who now ruefully regretted the acceptance of Thomas as a missionary. The doctor made a hasty journey to London to try and find the writer of the letter, but without avail, and he returned in time to join Carey in watching the fleet sail away.

This event, which appeared utterly disastrous to their hopes, turned out for the best. Repairing once more to London, Thomas heard of a Danish Indiaman daily expected in the Downs and bound for Serampore, a Danish settlement on the Hooghly, and beyond the jurisdiction of the dreaded East India Company. The agent demanded a high price for the passage, and without delay Fuller, Thomas, and Carey began a new campaign for collecting funds. Fuller canvassed the members of the London churches, and met with many rebuffs. One writer mentions "the touching picture of the strong, stern, great-souled man, footsore and disappointed, turning aside into a back lane to weep unseen."

Thomas and Carey went to Northamptonshire, where Thomas succeeded in inducing Mrs. Carey to join her husband. Encouraged by the example of Mrs. Thomas, the timid wife reluctantly consented on the condition that she should be accompanied by her sister. This swelled the passage money to £600, but in God's good providence, by begging and borrowing, it was secured, though it necessitated Carey's selling a small property ; and within twenty-four hours of his wife's consent he was on his way to London with his family. They were welcomed to the ship by Captain Christmas, the commander of the vessel, and sailed for the East on the 13th June 1793, never to see England again.

The voyage was long and uncomfortable, though

comparatively uneventful. Poor Mrs. Carey had scarcely left England before she commenced her ceaseless reproaches. The fare on board was coarse and unappetising, and Thomas was a source of much disquietude. Carey's estimate of him was expressed in the words: "a man of sterling worth, but perhaps of the most singular make of any man in the world." A frivolous and argumentative Frenchman, a deist, was among the passengers, and annoyed the missionaries with his banter; but their evident earnestness greatly impressed the Danish and Norwegian sailors. The captain was an earnest Christian, of whom Carey wrote that he was "one of the most polite, accomplished gentlemen who ever sustained the name of a sea-captain."

A storm near the Cape of Good Hope proved an anxious time, when the great Antarctic rollers appeared like mountains to the inexperienced landsmen. In the Indian Ocean a close look-out had to be kept for pirates, numbers of whom were fitted out in Mauritius, and were a continual menace to shipping in the southern seas. But through it all Carey was upheld by the remembrance of the men who were praying for him in England; and his mind was continually occupied with the dire need in the lands of darkness. Seated in the tiny cabin, gazing out, ever and anon, over the restless waters, he wrote to the Committee: "I hope the Society will go on and increase, and that the multitude of heathen in the world may hear the glorious words of truth. Africa" (the immense length of which he was experiencing) "is but a little way from England—Madagascar but a little farther; South America, and all the Numerous and Large islands in the Indian and Chinese Seas, I hope will not be passed over. A large field opens

on every side." What a man this was who penned
such words at a time when the Church as a whole
cared for none of these things, and when even his
own Committee thought their entrance into Bengal a
remarkable venture of faith!

After a brief call at a port on the east coast of India,
they reached the Hooghly early in November 1793,
and as Carey and his party watched the faint verge
of green deepen into belts and groves of cocoanut palms,
his earnest longing found expression in the words:
" O may my heart be prepared for our work, and the
Kingdom of Christ be set up among these poor
Hindus."

Thus, the apostle who was prevented from going to
Africa or Tahiti, as had been his desire, was led to the
centre of British rule in India, the most strategic point
of that day in the whole foreign field, and carried
thither on a ship bound for Serampore, by means of
which the party were enabled to enter Calcutta unnoticed.   Glancing back over the series of events that
led Carey to this point in his lifework, we are conscious
again of the guiding hand of God, by whom were all
things arranged and to whose glory they all tended.

CHAPTER V.

INDIA AS CAREY FOUND IT.

"The East bowed low before the blast
In patient, deep disdain ;
She let the legions thunder past,
Then plunged in thought again."
                                MATTHEW ARNOLD.

INDIA—it is not a country, but a continent; a continent with twenty nations and twice as many languages, a world in itself.

From time immemorial there have flowed in upon India invading armies from the hardier and less fertile lands of Central Asia, each new conqueror bringing destruction, rapine, and cruel suffering in his train. In the intervals between the conquests, when the last invaders had succumbed to the enervating influences of Hindostan, there would arise princes of the land, puissant and bloodthirsty as those from the outer world, princes with rule as heavy and degrading as that of the foreigners. To the unresisting myriads of India it mattered little who reigned at Delhi, for tyranny and oppression was their constant lot.

The real history of India began when Mahmoud of Ghazni led his warriors over the snowy passes of the north-west to conquer the peninsula. But as the centuries rolled away, the conquerors became the conquered, overcome by the voluptuousness of the

Photo by]

SURAT, THE CRADLE OF BRITISH POWER IN INDIA.

[E. A. Annett.

climate and the debasing vices that they practised; and the land became a great battlefield where rival kings fought with each other for a share in the crumbling empire.

Then came the ships of Europe. First were the Portuguese, and with them Francis Xavier, who with a heart of fire but a hand of steel planted Roman Catholicism along the south-west seaboard. The British followed, first as traders to Surat in the west, and then to Fort St. David in the south, whence British arms first began to overthrow all comers. Later a station was opened on the Hooghly, and there, after many vicissitudes, Fort William began to be the centre of British dominance. They came to trade, but they stayed to rule; commerce developed into conquest, and by the daring and the genius of a handful of strong men they rescued India from her long internecine strife, and they gave this land of age-long suffering peace and something approaching a national life.

There were many tragedies writ deep in the memories of men of all nations in Hindostan, mistakes made and retrieved at great cost; but out of these has risen an empire in which the Indian nations are blending into one and the land is prospering as never before. The labourer at last can claim justice equally with the landowner, and the inhabitants have lived for so long in peace that they have begun to forget that there ever were wrongs and tyrannies and awful deeds of blood.

But that was not yet—the East India Company still ruled when Carey landed. The battle of Plassey, which had transformed the Company from merchants into viceroys, exposed its servants to the temptations

of absolute power. A boundless field for the gratification of ambition and avarice was opened before them,
and for a time every feeling of Christian virtue was
sacrificed to the accumulation of wealth. Although
the records of those days enshrine the memories of
isolated men who preserved a true faith in God and
who exhibited a care for the spiritual welfare of their
fellow-subjects, the Company sternly forbade any
attempt at evangelisation, and even upheld the temples
of the land by their favour and pecuniary support.
The directors plainly showed their antipathy to any
form of missionary effort, not hesitating even to give
expression to it before the British Parliament.

"The conversion of five hundred or a thousand
Hindus," they urged, "would be the most serious
disaster that could happen;" and they thanked God
that it was impracticable. They affirmed that the
higher and more respectable natives were of the purest
morality and the most sterling virtue; that the project
of converting them to Christianity was the most wild,
extravagant, expensive, and unjustifiable project that
was ever suggested by the most visionary speculator.

These were the men who held the monopoly of
governing India's destinies, and who were determined
that the Bible should be kept out of the land so that
England might the more thoroughly drain its resources.
And this was the implacable opposition that Carey
and his fellows had to fight against for nearly thirty
years.

There had been previous attempts at evangelisation,
but almost entirely in the south. There the early
Danish missionaries Ziegenbalg and Plutschau, and
afterwards Schwartz and his colleagues, financed from
Britain, had done a great and enduring work. But

Carey was the first ordained British missionary to reach India, and in Bengal and the north he had no predecessor from any land. Kiernander had come to Bengal from the south at the instance of Clive, but his efforts were mainly confined to the Portuguese Eurasians, and little resulted from his general work.

From the moral standpoint, despite the affirmations of the Company's directors, India was in a state loudly calling for help. " A foul mythology, a saddening demon worship, and an exacting social system covered the land as with a pall." Carey found around him on every hand temples and shrines of Vishnu, Ganesh, the elephant-headed son of Siva the Destroyer, of Siva himself, and especially of Kali or Durga, his frightful consort.

In the first chapter of the Epistle to the Romans, speaking of the degradation of man in words that burn their way into the soul, the Apostle Paul says: " professing themselves to be wise, they became fools, and changed the glory of the incorruptible God into an image made like corruptible man, and to birds, and four-footed beasts, and creeping things." Such a summary might apply to the religion of ancient India, where the peacock, the cow, and the monkey were worshipped. But the Hindus had gone farther, much farther than this, for they had changed the glory of God into the image of demons, to whom, even as they bowed before them, they attributed the most soul-debasing vices, and in whose worship lust ran riot.

The chief shrine of Calcutta, after which the very town is probably named, is Kali Ghat. Here Kali is still presented as a giantess; her jewels are the bones of her victims, men's bodies her earrings, the skulls of men whose lives she has taken her necklace; her only garment is a girdle of dead men's hands about her loins; her eyes are red as a drunkard's, her tongue protrudes, her breasts are smeared with blood. A four-armed creature, in one hand she holds at arm's length the head of the husband she slew. And to this image came the mothers of Calcutta and brought their babes to worship the abomination with their faces in the dust. Priests stood by, men who had fathomed every vice and discarded every virtue, while the neighbouring houses sheltered hardened women and little girls, the ministrants of vice. Hideous "holy men" abounded, dressed up with the childish object of outvying each other in absurdity. In Carey's time murderers and thieves openly appeared before the goddess to ask her help in their violence.

The tense indictment in Romans continues: "Wherefore God gave them up to uncleanness through the lust of their own hearts, to dishonour their own bodies between themselves; who exchanged the truth of God for a lie. . . ." These words seem as if especially written for India, and the truth of them was painfully in evidence on every hand. The stucco and granite carvings of the temples and the rude red drawings on the whitewashed walls were unspeakably abominable. No man, woman, or child could even approach some of the most renowned shrines of the land without defilement of mind.

In the earlier writings there were gems of beauty and spiritual worth enough to show a sense of God among the sages of those days, fragments that are exhibited to-day with justifiable pride by Hindus, and that are altogether exaggerated in importance by a class of European scholars. But such was not the religion that influenced and swayed the teeming multitudes into whose midst had come the undaunted messenger of the gospel.

There was needed a man to stand in the gap, a man to come to the help of the Lord against the mighty. And see, he has come—a little man, self-taught, with hard, horny hands, old for the task of learning of a new tongue, prematurely bald with the effects of fever. And the mighty are on every side, despising and contemptuous. William Carey has stepped on to Indian soil in the name of the Lord, and thrown down the gage of battle. A command from the unseen God, a book unknown to the sages of the East, an unquenchable love and an indomitable zeal are his weapons. India is enough to frighten him, but he refused to be frightened. He feared GOD, but he feared nothing else in heaven or earth. What will be the issue?

CHAPTER VI.

CALCUTTA.

"A HERO? I don't quite know what that is. But I imagine a
hero is a man who does what he can. The others do not."
ROMAINE ROLAND in *Jean Christophe.*

THE little party landed in Calcutta unnoted by the
Government and, indeed, unnoticed by everybody.
Thomas, as an old resident, took charge of arrangements,
and a comfortable house was secured for the two
families.

They were visited almost at once by Ram Bosu, an
intelligent Bengali teacher who had come under
Thomas's influence years before. He had given great
promise as an inquirer, but when left alone he had
gone back to his idols. Now, however, he gladly
joined himself to the household, full of penitence for
his fall, and as he had a smattering of English, Carey
gladly engaged him as a pundit. To Thomas was
given the work of housekeeping, while Carey devoted
himself to Bengali, making rapid progress with the
language.

The funds they had brought out for their support
were invested in goods, as this was then considered
the most advantageous method. The disposal of these
was entrusted to Thomas, who was supposed to understand the Calcutta market. Difficulties soon arose,
however, for Thomas was as thriftless as he was un-

businesslike, and in an expensive place like Calcutta, the money disappeared as rapidly as it came in.

It soon became clear that they must find a cheaper residence, and they therefore removed to Bandel, about twenty-five miles up the river. Here they met the venerable Kiernander, who greatly cheered Carey by his unabated ardour, though he was now too old for active service. Bandel was found to offer few advantages for their Mission, and they moved on to Nuddea, a stronghold of Brahmanism and a fine centre for work.

The preachers were welcomed by the religious teachers, with whom they had considerable influence. "We seem inclined to settle here," wrote Carey, "as it is the bulwark of Hinduism, which, if once carried, all the country must be laid open before us." His idea was, "to build me a hut, and live like the natives," but they found no ground in the neighbourhood suitable for agriculture, and they soon returned to Calcutta, where they heard there was waste land to be obtained freely from the Government. In this they were disappointed, and Thomas's creditors compelled him to take up his profession again to meet their demands. Carey now heard of an appointment vacant in the Botanical Gardens and eagerly applied for it, only to find that it had just been filled up.

The poor man was at his wits' end, for they were homeless and almost penniless in this great Eastern city. His wife already showed signs of mental aberration, and bitterly reproached him for their distressful condition. His children were seized with dysentery, the result of six weeks of exposure and unsuitable food up the river. The Committee on which they relied was far away, and there was always the fear before him that the Government might deport them from the country.

In his extremity God raised up a friend in the person of a wealthy native, a money-lender, who had made advances to Thomas. This man offered them, until they could do better, the use of a garden house

A CALCUTTA BURNING GHAT.

in his grounds in Manicktolla, a suburb of the town. The place was miserably small and ill-ventilated, and without any of the conveniences necessary to the health of Europeans in the tropics, but it was a great boon at such a time. Carey never forgot the banker's kindness, and it was a great joy to him, twenty years later, to be able to give material assistance to this very man when a sudden change of circumstances had reduced him to poverty.

To appreciate the hardships of Carey's position at this time, and to gain a due estimate of the narrative of his habits in the years to follow, let us take a glance at Calcutta life of the period.

The European community, composed almost entirely of officials and merchants, lived in mansions on Chowringhee, the fashionable street facing the river. Salaries were large and furloughs infrequent, so that money was spent with prodigality. We have but to read the bill of fare of a dinner-table to see the way in which the Europeans of that day indulged themselves. A lady writing from Calcutta a few years before the arrival of Carey, says: "Wine is the heaviest family article, for whether it is taken fashionably or medicinally, every lady drinks at least a bottle per day, and the gentlemen four times that quantity." It is not surprising that she adds: " The ladies retire after dinner (two o'clock) not to enjoy their private chat, for to sleep is the object of their wishes and the occupation of their time—a refreshment that alone enables them to appear with animation in the evening." It may be said that English claret, the cheapest of the wines used, cost at this time £6 per dozen.

At sunset Calcutta was all animation with society, which came out for its airing. Chariots and phaetons of English build were common, and high officials drove their four-in-hands. The ladies would have "their horses finely set out with silver nets to guard their necks from insects, and reins elegantly decorated. . . . To finish the whole a kind of umbrella is suspended not infrequently over the lady's head, which gives her the true Eastern grandeur of appearance." On the river, pinnaces, many-oared and magnificent, were then the fashion, and families thus disported themselves.

Some of these carried bands of music, and the extravagant youth affected African slaves.

The evenings were spent visiting, every house was open and refreshment served liberally. Supper would be at ten, with card-parties following, lasting till midnight. Large sums of money were lost at these. Mr. Philip Francis, the foe of Warren Hastings, acknowledged winning £20,000 at whist in a few weeks (report said the sum was much larger). Dancing was carried to such an excess that many ladies were said to have gone into consumption as a result.

In the cool season hunting was much indulged in. The expense of living was very high. A member of one household wrote : " Our house-keeping costs £500 a year, with 110 servants to wait on us, a family of 4 people, and we are economists." Sir Elijah Impey told how he had not been able to lay up more than £3000 in any year. We scarcely wonder that Carey writes concerning Europeans of " their profuse way of living ! "

Contentment seems to have been less easily obtained. Macaulay, writing a little later, voiced the general feelings of ennui when he said : " We have our share of the miseries of life in this country. We are annually baked four months, boiled four more, and allowed the remaining four to get cool if we can. Insects and undertakers are the only living creatures which seem to enjoy the climate. . . . All the fruits of the tropics are not worth a bottle of Covent Garden strawberries, and a lodging up three pairs of stairs in London is better than a palace in a compound in Chowringhee."

Sabbath desecration was common, and the day was given up almost entirely to horse-racing and gambling.

The secretary of Philip Francis wrote in 1775: "We are upon excellent terms with the clergy here. They are not numerous, but thoroughly orthodox. One rivals Nimrod in hunting, a second supplies bullocks for the army, another is a perfect connoisseur in Chinese gardening. I endeavour to obtain some light from them all, but the fear of God is not the kind of wisdom most in regard in Bengal." The Governor-General wrote officially in 1795: "Our clergy in Bengal, with some exceptions, are not respectable characters." He added that from the general relaxation of morals, "A black coat is no security."

But the clergy were very few. In North India at the time there were fifty stations, and most of them had never had a minister of religion; while in Bengal in 1806, with 13,000 Protestants, there were only three churches. One of the exceptions noted by the Governor-General was the Rev. David Brown, who arrived in 1786 as pastor for orphan children of military officers and men. He was a man of great piety and character, and, later, he had the support of the prominent chaplain, Claudius Buchanan,—both of these ultimately becoming fast friends of Carey and his fellows.

During the years immediately before Carey reached India there had been a fine band of Christian gentlemen in Calcutta—Grant, Udny, and their friends; and these, with the example of the Marquis of Wellesley and the assistance of Brown and afterwards of Buchanan and Carey, did great things towards developing a higher ideal of public life and personal morality.

We left our hero and his family, seven persons in all, living in the tiny and uncomfortable garden house of Nellu Das, the banker, at Manicktolla. Their distress was now greater than they had ever known.

Money they had none, except as they could wring a little out of Thomas. Mrs. Carey constantly upbraided her husband with being the cause of their wretchedness, and contrasted their poverty with the comparative luxury in which the Thomases lived, though on borrowed money. Dysentery became chronic with most of them, and their sufferings were very great.

Carey would not have been allowed by the authorities to remain in Calcutta as a missionary, but few were aware of the existence of the obscure vagrant, as he seemed. In spite of fears and temptations to despond, the missionary kept his faith steadfastly on his Master, and persevered marvellously with the language. Already he was able to address the Mohammedans and Hindoos around, and with Ram Bosu to help him, he daily went out to the public thoroughfares to preach and explain the gospel. Never for a moment did he lose sight of the object of his coming to India. Already he had commenced his great work of translation, and had finished the correction of the early chapters of Genesis.

Two extracts from his journal made at this time give us a glimpse of his spirited labour and of the hardness of his way: " . . . was very weary, having walked in the sun about fifteen or sixteen miles, yet had the satisfaction of discussing with some money-changers who could speak English."

The second concerns his first call on David Brown. "He received me," says Carey, "with cool politeness. I stayed near an hour with him; found him a very sensible man, but a marked disgust prevails, on both sides, between him and Mr. Thomas. He carried himself as greatly my superior. and I left him without his having so much as asked me to take any refreshment, though he knew I had walked five miles in the heat of the sun."

It is difficult for us to realise what these long hours of tramping in the hot, steaming air of Calcutta meant to the man who, with his family, was on the verge of starvation.

"High in the fierce, blue heavens, the great white sun is burning—
He has shone, so it seems to me, for a year of days and more—
I am sick of the blinding glare, and my dizzy brain is turning,
As his quivering streamers dance on city and sea and shore.
O that a cloud would rise—the terrible splendour veiling—
Blot him out of my sight, if but for an hour's short space !
But never the faintest speck is seen in the azure sailing,
Still from the pitiless blue he mocks me with dazzling face." [1]

It was when things were at their darkest that suddenly there arose a gleam of hope, and, as before, it came from an unexpected quarter. Ram Bosu, who knew Carey's desire to take up land for agricultural purposes, proposed that they should go to the Sunderbunds—tiger-haunted swamps to the south-east of Calcutta, where his uncle was a zemindar, and where land could be easily obtained.

Carey grasped eagerly at the idea, and with considerable difficulty Thomas borrowed for him the sum of £16 from a native lender. With this a boat was hired and Carey with his family embarked on it, leaving Calcutta behind him with heartfelt relief.

[1] From *In the Tropics*, by Margaret Macdonald.

CHAPTER VII.

PERILS IN THE WILDERNESS.

"Are they ministers of Christ? I more; in labours more abundant, in deaths oft, in journeyings often, in perils of waters, in perils in the wilderness."—THE APOSTLE PAUL.

BENGAL is a vast alluvial plain, watered and fertilised by the Ganges and the Brahmaputra which bring down a constant flood from the mighty Himalayas. Over the land is a network of waterways, and along these are chiefly concentrated the dense population of this favoured part of India.

To the south and south-east of Calcutta spreads out towards the sea the enormous Delta—the Sunderbunds, a tract of 6000 square miles facing the Bay of Bengal. Once this had been populous and prosperous, but because of the incursions of pirates it was now deserted jungle, the haunt of tigers and other wild beasts, and a veritable hot-bed of malaria. The Government had recently attempted to reclaim this fertile land, but much of it still remained a pestilential wilderness, in which it was almost certain death for an unacclimatised European to reside.

Ignorant of the deadly character of the district, the Carey family left Calcutta in a native boat—a long, open canoe, fitted with a tiny deck-house. By day the sun beat down upon them in its intensity, and by night they shivered with the chill of the river

and listened with dread to the roaring of wild animals.
For three days they journeyed, going they knew not
whither, at times skirting dense jungle, and again
running for miles along low ground reeking with
deadly miasma. On the fourth day, with their provisions reduced to barely sufficient for another meal,

NATIVE CRAFT ON THE GANGES DELTA.

they began to lose hope. It seemed as if they had
come to the wilderness to die.

At this juncture a bend of the river brought into
view the bungalow of a European. It was the
residence of Mr. Charles Short, a salt-inspector, a
minor official of the Government, and this gentleman
welcomed the miserable family and their stout-hearted
father to his home. With a fine spirit of hospitality
he invited them to remain with him for six months, or

even longer, until they could find a suitable place to settle in. In belief their host proved to be a deist, but he was so deeply impressed by the fine faith of his visitor that he became truly converted to Christ. He eventually married Mrs. Carey's sister, who still accompanied them.

At Hasnabad, "the smiling spot," not far away, Carey took a few acres on the bank of the stream, and at once commenced to build his house. "The Walls," he wrote, "will be made with mats fastened to Posts of Wood, and the roof with Bamboo and Thatched." Such was the first home the emissaries of the gospel built in Bengal, no lofty rooms and wide-spreading verandahs as are considered essential to health in such a climate, but a cottage of the kind used to-day by the Government for the temporary assistance of Indian labourers driven from their homes by the dreaded plague.

Carey was, however, in the best of spirits. "The country," he wrote, "is an excellent soil, but has lately been deserted upon account of Tygers and other Beasts of Prey which infest the place; but all are afraid of a Gun, and will be soon expelled. The people therefore will not be afraid, though they have kept from others because they think Englishmen are worse than Tygers (!) We shall have all the necessaries of Life except bread, for which rice must be a substitute. Wild hogs, deers, and Fowls are to be procured by the Gun, and must supply us with a considerable part of our food, and in the woods there are Rhinoceros's which are good food, but it is dangerous going after them for fear of Tygers."

The house was slowly completed. "So much of my time," he writes, "is taken up in procuring provisions and cultivating my little farm." Confiding in the missionary's gun against the tigers and in his kindliness towards themselves, a number of natives came and settled around, so that the place soon took on the aspect of a little town. By his unwearied industry he had made such good progress with the language that he was able now to talk with ease in Bengali, of which he says, " I find it an easy language."

But things went hardly with them. His family were still ill with dysentery, nor likely to improve in such a situation. No word reached them from the Committee, who themselves had to wait fourteen long months before they received their first news of those they had sent forth. Difficulties and discouragements abounded, and yet the man remained the same in his intense love for the world that lay in darkness.

"I think the Society would do well," he wrote from the dreadful Sunderbunds, " if they would still keep their eye towards Africa or Asia. These countries are not like the wilds of America where long labour will scarce collect sixty people to hear the word. For here it is almost impossible to go out of the way of hundreds, and preachers are wanted a thousand times more than people to preach to."

Yet despite these sturdy words, the Mission that had been launched with such great enthusiasm and high hopes now found itself on the malarious banks of a jungle stream, surrounded by but a few despised villagers, and far from all that would appear as a strategic or even a favourable centre for operations. But God had not forgotten His servants. An unexpected change was at hand.

Mr. Udny, an earnest Christian gentleman, who in the earlier days had helped to support Mr. Thomas, was now in charge of the East India Company's commercial factory at Malda, a station 400 miles north of Calcutta. Acquainted with Thomas's needy state he now kindly offered him the charge of a newly-opened indigo factory near Malda, and hearing from Thomas of Carey's situation, he sent an offer of a similar post to him. The position carried with it a salary of £250 a year and a prospect of a share in the turnover. Carey was delighted with a proposal that not only rescued him and his family from starvation, but which opened up a field of wide usefulness, freed from the fear of Government opposition.

They were soon on their way north, all eager for the change. To Carey the slow journey was an opportunity for spreading the gospel. "Were the superstitions of the heathen a million times more than they are," he records, "God's cause will triumph." "I will most certainly publish the Bible," he wrote joyfully, on his arrival at Mudnabatty, his new home; and in the letter to Mr. Fuller, he asks that now, as he will no longer require support from England, they will send a man to Sumatra with the money they would have used for India. "I wish you also to send me out," he added, "a few instruments of husbandry, viz., scythes, sickles, plough wheels, and such things, and a yearly assortment of all garden and flowering seeds . . . for the advantage of the country I now call my own." He also assured them that it would be his joy to remain in the same relation to them as if he were receiving his allowance direct from them.

This letter produced a painful impression on the Committee in England. His dearest friends, even, were afraid that he was swerving from his original purpose. The Committee resolved, "That though, on the whole,

we cannot disapprove of the conduct of our brethren
in their late engagement, yet, considering the frailty of
human nature in the best of men, a letter of serious
and affectionate caution be addressed to them." This
resolution appears rather uncalled for when it is remembered that the missionaries were expected to earn
their own living, and that so small an amount of
money had hitherto been sent out for their support.

Carey's feelings were wounded by the letter from the
Committee, and in his journal we find the following
record: "One part . . . surprised me; I mean that
respecting our engaging in employment for our support.
I always understood that the Society recommended
it. . . . To vindicate my own spirit or conduct I should
be very averse. It is a constant maxim with me that
if my conduct will not vindicate itself, it is not worth
vindicating; but we really thought we were acting in
conformity with the universal wishes of the Society.
Whether we are indolent or laborious, or whether the
spirit of the missionary is swallowed up in the pursuits
of the merchant, it becomes me not to say; but our
labours will speak for us. I only say that, after our
family's obtaining a bare allowance, my whole income
goes for the purposes of the gospel. . . . I am indeed
poor, and shall always be so till the Bible is published
in Bengali and Hindustani, and the people want no
further instruction."

CHAPTER VIII.

THE INDIGO MERCHANT.

"I am made all things to all men, that I might by all means save some."—THE APOSTLE PAUL.

MUDNABATTY was an insignificant village of two-score homes, lying near the bank of a small river. The inhabitants were very poor, being engaged mostly as agricultural labourers in the indigo and rice fields near at hand. The plain was unrelieved by any hill, and the jungle lay in dark patches in every direction.

At the season of the year when Carey first came to his new home, Nature was at her best, for the needy earth had grown lovely with the slaking of her great thirst. The monsoon showers had washed the air, and the pale green shoots of the rice were showing in the glistening water, and maize and millet waved in the breeze.

Carey found the work of the factory more congenial than his occupation in England, and laboured with his usual thoroughness to make the venture successful. The closest attention had to be paid to it for three months of the year, but during the remaining nine months the work was light. Constant journeys were needful over the surrounding district, and these gave him the opportunity of an intimate acquaintance with the manners and customs of the people. His letters of this period abound in most reliable observations on all that concerned the life, religions, habits, and manufactures of Bengal, and serve to indicate the broad views he took of the welfare of the country to which he had devoted himself.

The factory itself and all its arrangements he endeavoured to conduct on Christian principles, believing that the evidence of truthfulness, fairness, and righteousness in business would commend the gospel to all who were connected with him. He daily assembled the servants and labourers of the factory, ninety persons in all, for Christian worship, though he exercised the utmost care to avoid anything that might savour of coercion in the matter of conscience. No one could have been more particular than he in this respect. Nothing of worldly advantage was held out to those he sought to win, and it was a continual source of pain to him to find that men and women came with professions of interest in his teaching in order to secure pecuniary assistance or advancement. The conviction of the sacredness of conscience, even in a heathen, determined his whole method of dealing with the people.

His district for trade occupied an area of twenty square miles, with a total of more than two hundred villages, among which he unceasingly preached the gospel. With great eagerness he seized upon every opportunity for direct missionary service. Schools for the village children were opened, the first of the kind in North India, and a dispensary which entailed a large and constant expense was carried on at his residence. English services were found possible in some places, and in one of these the assistant judge of the district was converted, greatly to Carey's encouragement. This gentleman remained for many years a stalwart friend of the Mission.

In his own home Carey laboured on at his work of Bible translation, and finding that Sanskrit would be useful to him in the furtherance of his literary projects, he applied himself with the utmost diligence to the acquirement of this, the mother tongue of the Aryan peoples. Not a stone was left unturned in his efforts for the evangelisation of the country.

He found the simple people around him very willing to listen to his preaching; but though it "was easy to confound their arguments," he sorrowfully remarks "their hearts remained the same." Occasionally he had Brahmans and others of high caste in his audience, and rejoiced at the opportunity of discoursing with them. Conciliatory and tactful as ever was his method, he nevertheless spoke with great directness. On one occasion a young Brahman spent two hours vainly endeavouring to entangle the preacher, and at the end was met with the plain words, "Brahman, you know that you have used every crooked argument in your power to support your cause, notwithstanding which you are involved in inextricable difficulty. Why will you adhere to so bad a cause?" He then spoke to him of Jesus Christ, and prayed so earnestly that the young man acknowledged that his heart had gone with the prayer. Such things happened frequently, and gave hope of fruit.

Of all the customs of Hinduism, that which weighed most heavily upon him was the inhuman practice of suttee, whereby the widow was burned on the funeral pyre of her husband. The first time he witnessed a suttee burning was on a return journey from Calcutta. Seeing a concourse of people on the bank of the river, he went towards them, and to his horror found that a widow was about to ascend the stack of wood faggots upon which lay the body of her husband. He first inquired whether the deed was purely voluntary on the part of the woman, and being assured that this was the case, he reasoned and remonstrated with her and with her relatives. It was all of no avail, and thereupon, in agonised tones, he exclaimed against the act as one of shocking murder. The widow, exhorted by the priests, calmly ascended the pile, utterly ignoring his entreaties. Inflammable material was heaped above her, and she was pinned down by strong bamboos; and as the fire was lit, any groans or screams were rendered inaudible by the excited shouts of the spectators.

Threatening to testify against them at the judgment seat of God, Carey rushed away filled with horror and shame. He determined that in every way possible he would strive for the abolition of so inhuman a practice, and he did not rest until, many years later, the Governor-General passed a law absolutely prohibiting suttee.

Meanwhile his translation of the Bengali Testament was speeding on, and after nearly four years of intense and careful labour he had the joy of bringing the task to completion. The next step was to have it printed, but here a great difficulty arose. The only printing presses in the country were in Calcutta, and in the hands of avaricious Europeans, who expected as enormous profits from their business as were secured in other branches of trade. The estimate given him for printing 10,000 copies on coarse native paper, exclusive of binding, was £4400, a sum far beyond all Carey's dreams. It may be noted that the price of

10,000 New Testaments to-day in India, printed on good paper and bound, would be under £80!

Driven by this obstacle to form a fresh plan, he wrote to the Committee proposing that they should send from England a set of Bengali type, punches, a press, a supply of paper, and " a serious printer." His ardent spirit ill brooked the delay that would be necessary before he could hope for even a reply to his request. It was therefore with great delight that he heard of a wooden press offered for sale in Calcutta at the low price of £40, and he lost no time in making the purchase. Mr. Udny, who had ever taken a deep interest in Carey's labours, claimed the privilege of presenting the press to the Mission, and before long it was set up in a side room in the factory. The people came in great numbers to see the strange machine and to hear of its wonderful powers. The general decision they arrived at was that it was a European idol!

In 1796 the family was unexpectedly joined at Mudnabatty by John Fountain, a young man well recommended by the Committee. He had entered the country unnoticed by the authorities, having rated himself as a ship's servant. He was unfortunately a man of small attainments and of less energy, and added little to the strength of the Mission. He had imbibed the views of the French revolutionists, and was in the habit of using such unbridled language that it was found necessary by the Committee to threaten him with recall if he failed to restrain himself. Thus Carey's second associate was but a disappointment to him.

Occasionally his itineracy took him far afield beyond the limits of his district. In 1797, in company with Thomas, he made a journey to Bhutan, whose stupendous, snow-clad mountains could be seen from near his bungalow. Carey's account of his meeting with the Soobah, the native governor of this independent state, is most interesting.

"The genuine politeness of the Soobah," he wrote, "exceeded everything that can be imagined, and his generosity was astonishing. He insisted on supplying all our people with everything they wanted; and if we did but cast our eyes to any object in the room, he immediately presented us with one of the same sort. He presented each of us that night with a sword, shield, helmet, and cup made of very light, beautiful wood. We admiring the wood, he gave us a large log of it, which appeared to be like fir, with a very dark, beautiful grain; it is full of resin, and burns like a candle if cut in thin pieces. In eating, the Soobah imitated our manners so quickly and exactly that though he had never seen a European before, yet he appeared as free as if he had spent his life with them. We ate his food—but rather sparingly. We had much talk about the gospel."

Then, after telling of a public honour the Soobah did them, he adds: "Being seated in the market-place, we exchanged five rupees and five pieces of betel, in the sight of the whole town; and having chewed betel for the first time in our lives, we embraced three times in the Eastern manner and then shook hands in the English manner, after which he made us a present of a piece of rich debang wrought with gold, each a Bhutan blanket and a tail of an animal called the cheer cow as brushy as a horse's. In the morning he brought us more presents and sent us away with every honour: as a band of music before, guides to show us the way, etc." Carey maintained a friendly correspondence with the Soobah for some time afterwards, and never ceased to hope for the establishment of a mission there.

Mudnabatty, however, was no place for Europeans to live in. The low grounds around the village were annually flooded by the rains, and converted into a pestiferous marsh. Fever and dysentery were abundant, and Carey himself was very severely attacked by both of these disorders, returning with slow and feeble steps from the very gates of death. His little son, Peter, died from fever, and the event, besides being a heavy trial to Carey himself, proved altogether too much for his poor wife. She was smitten with incurable melancholia, and had to be kept under restraint thenceforward to her dying day. The burdened man wrote to a friend: "I have very sore trials in my own family, from a quarter which I forbear to mention."

In his loneliness Carey longed for true associates, but the jealousy with which the East India Company guarded the land from interlopers presented a great obstacle. In 1783 the British Parliament had been induced to decree that if any subject of His Majesty should without licence be found in the East Indies he should be liable to fine or imprisonment. In 1793 the penalty had been mitigated to deportation. This power had on the whole been used with moderation, but it pressed very heavily on those who wished to be missionaries, since they were peculiarly obnoxious to the Company.

Despite the initial difficulty of securing an entrance, Carey proposed to the Committee to found a settlement on the Moravian model, composed of several families. The wives were to be as hearty in the work as the husbands, and the families were to live together and have all things in common. The settlement was to be of small straw houses built in a square. One or two stewards were to be appointed to manage the affairs, and there were to be fixed rules regarding eating, drinking, sleeping, and working. The cost was estimated at £40 a month for half a dozen families living in this style.

The primitive simplicity and self-denial of the plan were a better testimony to Carey's zeal and devotion than to his soundness of judgment. Such a colony would have gone to pieces within a twelvemonth, for life there would be impossible for Europeans under such conditions. Fuller, however, agreed with the proposal in the main, and advised Carey to see the Governor-General and ask his approval. Lord Wellesley simply smiled at it, and told Carey that the thing was impossible, if for no other reason, for this: that no missionary, as such, was legally allowed to reside in the country.

The matter was soon settled in a manner little expected by Carey or the Committee. The indigo factory was not prospering, chiefly because of the ill-chosen site and the frequent floods; and Mr. Udny felt compelled to relinquish it. The Committee, when the news reached them, responded warmly, and re-solved to pay Carey the arrears of the allowance he had declined some years before, and to leave the mode of future maintenance to his discretion. Anticipating the closing of Mudnabatty, Carey purchased another small factory for £300, hoping by this means to provide funds for the Mission. Here he immediately set about erecting buildings for his model settlement in the hope of early reinforcements from England. His business ability, however, was small; and bitter hostility was shown to him by Mr. Udny's successor. The little money he possessed was soon fruitlessly expended.

It was five years now since he had arrived at Mudnabatty, and they had been years full of pecuniary anxiety. Had he not worked for his living, indeed, he must have starved, for supplies from England were meagre. Amid the many discouragements, Carey had found it difficult to continue in a hopeful spirit. "I preach every day to the natives," he says; "I try to speak of Jesus Christ and Him crucified, and of Him alone; but my soul is often much dejected to see no fruit." "For the first seven years of my stay in this country," he wrote a little later, "my mind was almost dried up by discouragement and want of success. I then felt spiritless, and went to the work like a soldier who only expected to be defeated."

Yet he ever persisted; he fainted not nor failed. Though he had not seen one convert for all his labours, the elemental greatness of the man was shown in the strength of his dogged perseverance, allied to a love for humanity that knew no bounds, and a devotion to Christ that was absolute. He had learnt never to count a cause as lost when GOD was behind it. Moreover, the experience gained had been of great value as a preparation for future work.

CHAPTER IX.

REINFORCEMENTS.

"Send me anywhere, provided it be forward."
DAVID LIVINGSTONE.

THE long-prayed-for reinforcements at length arrived. Marshman, Daniel Brunsdon, William Grant, with their wives, William Ward, and Miss Todd, who was to marry Mr. Fountain, reached the Hooghly in October 1799. Owing to the great difficulty in obtaining a passage from England, they had come by way of America and in an American ship, commanded by another Christian gentleman, Captain Wickes. Their intention was to proceed to Mudnabatty and settle with Carey.

Instead of landing in Calcutta, they put off from the ship with their luggage in small boats, and, acting on advice given them in England, they rowed all night up the river, reaching Serampore at dawn the following day. It was Sunday morning when they landed, and Serampore was looking its best. Sixteen miles above Calcutta, the river here is still half a mile wide, and of great beauty. The houses of Serampore are hidden away among bright peepul and tamarind trees, while overhead lordly palms wave with the slightest zephyr. Across the river is Barrackpore, the magnificent country seat of the Governor-General of Bengal.

Serampore was at that time a Danish settlement, and a place of considerable importance. It was one of the small trading stations which, dotted along the Indian coast, displayed the flag of some European country and were under the protection of the nation they represented. It had risen greatly in value since the battle of Plassey in 1757, until it had gradually become the principal free port in Bengal. The stalwart Danish governors had been forced to withstand many a diplomatic attempt on the part of the Bengal Government; and the Governor at this time, Colonel Bie, a man of piety and wide sympathy, had more than once given the Calcutta authorities to understand that he would brook no high-handed action on their part.

The new arrivals were disappointed at finding neither Carey nor Thomas to meet them, and they were greatly perturbed when Captain Wickes appeared with the news that his vessel might not be cleared until they had reported themselves at Calcutta. In dire perplexity, they called upon Colonel Bie, who received them warmly, and gave them a welcome to remain in Serampore as long as they wished. For the sake of peace, however, he advised them to send a memorial to Calcutta explaining their aims.

Seldom in all the years since has a party of new missionaries of greater promise set out for the field. Marshman came of old Nonconformist stock, dating back to the days of Cromwell, and his mother was a Protestant refugee from France. His direct education had been in a village school where the master did not profess to teach either writing or arithmetic; but, like Carey, he had ever had an insatiable desire for reading. His memory was most remarkable; he seemed able to call up for use almost anything he ever had taken the pains to learn or study. At an early age he was introduced to the art of weaving, and spent ten years of his life at the loom. They were years of increasing mental power and religious experience. While still a young man he accepted a mastership in a school in Bristol, and while in that town he joined the Baptists and attended lectures in the Baptist Bristol Academy.

Mrs. Marshman was as keen a missionary as her husband, and her sound judgment, blended with the most sincere piety, was a source of untold strength to their fellow-workers through nearly half a century.

Ward also came of a good Christian family. He had begun life as apprentice to a printer. At the close of his apprenticeship he undertook the editorial charge of the *Derby Mercury*, which soon became one of the most popular journals in the county. He was an eager politician, and developing republican views, he came into conflict with Government. Removing to Hull, he spent six strenuous years in that city as editor of a local paper, and acquired in this way a large view of men and things, great facility of composition, and those business habits which were of inestimable value to the Mission in after days.

Ward's keen enthusiasm in the matter of the abolition of slavery brought him into touch with some of the choice spirits of the time and led up to his conversion. At once he became an ardent preacher, and his meeting with Carey in 1793 directed his sympathies toward the foreign field. When some time later he offered for work in Bengal, he was gladly accepted by the Baptist Missionary Society.

Grant and Brunsdon did not live long enough to

leave an impression upon the work in India, but both were men of ability and promise.

The appeal to Calcutta enabled Captain Wickes to get his ship cleared, but it did not help the new missionaries very much, even though it was backed up by the powerful influence of Messrs. Brown and Buchanan. By a strange blunder, the newspapers had given the information that "four *Papist* missionaries" had arrived in a foreign ship. This, in the days of Napoleon, was quite sufficient to cause police interference. Finding that Colonel Bie had no intention of surrendering the new-comers, no further objection was raised to them remaining in Serampore, but they were clearly given to understand that they might settle in no place in British India. They hired a small house in Serampore, where each family had the accommodation of a tiny chamber. The small common room they used for meals and also for services on Sunday, in which Colonel Bie and other residents joined them. But the house was damp and most unhealthy, and before they had been on shore three weeks one of the little band, Mr. Grant, had died.

Carey in the meantime hearing of their arrival and of their unexpected difficulty, wrote at once to Lord Wellesley, the Governor-General, asking permission for them to come to him. This request arrived at a time when Lord Wellesley had become exasperated with the defiant attitude shown toward himself by the Calcutta newspaper editors, and was in no mood to consider the application, especially for a mission press. It was peremptorily refused.

The bewildered missionaries at Serampore were advised on every hand of the impossibility of settling in British territory. It was at this juncture that Colonel Bie came to the rescue with a most generous offer. They were to have full leave to settle in Serampore, build churches, open schools, start a press, itinerate in the country around, and he would promise them the protection of the Danish Government in all their efforts. Moreover, he offered to hand over to them funds he had collected for a church building, and assured them of the utmost freedom and liberality in the acquiring of property. "I have received them," he wrote to a friend, "as righteous men in the name of righteous men; and I shall never withhold good from them to whom it is due, when it is in the power of my hand to do it. I am happy in possessing them, and will be more so in seeing their number increase; as this world gives much mould whereof earthen vessels are made, but little dust that gold cometh from."

Provided with a Danish passport, Ward sped away to Mudnabatty to advise with Carey, and reached there unmolested. Telling of his arrival, he wrote: "At length I saw Carey! He is less altered than I expected; has rather more flesh than in England, and, blessed be God! he is a young man still!" The conference between them did not last long. Carey felt it a wrench to leave Mudnabatty, his work, property, and school, his church and inquirers; but the leading was clear, and the family was soon on its way to Serampore.

On the journey down the brethren stopped for a short stay in the Raj Mahal hills, and preached to the wild Santals, who sat before them armed with bows and arrows. Carey records: "I long to stay here and tell these social and untutored heathens the good news . . . from heaven. I have a strong persuasion that the

A BENGALI PREACHER.

By permission of]   [*Lee Memorial Mission, Calcutta.*

doctrine of a dying Saviour would, under the Holy
Spirit's influence, melt their hearts." This district,
many years after, witnessed the coming of vast numbers
into the fold of Christ, though Carey did not live to
see it.

"Carey's apprenticeship was over; his full apostolate
was now to begin." For thirty-four years he was to
labour here at Serampore. Smuggled into India at the
first in spite of the Company, starved in Calcutta and
befriended in charity by a Hindu, compelled to build
himself a hut in the jungle, glad to take a salary as an
indigo planter, and latterly forced to consider accepting
the protection of a Bhutan Buddhist, he now found a
home in the Danish settlement of Serampore.

He was delighted with Marshman and Ward. He
wrote of them: "Brother Ward is the very man we
wanted: he enters into the work with his whole
soul, . . . Brother Marshman is a prodigy of diligence
and prudence; learning the language is mere play to
him. . . ." The names of these two men are indis-
solubly linked with that of Carey, and the story of
their labours together is a romance. Seldom, if ever,
did three men serve together in such absolute harmony
for so long a space of time with such unselfishness and
loftiness of aim. Mrs. Carey being now hopelessly
insane, the fellowship of the recruits and the presence
of earnest Christian women must have been as new
life to the hardly-pressed man, already a veteran in
experience.

No time was lost in getting to work. First a suitable home had to be found; and as rents were
excessively high, they purchased a large house with
accommodation for all, a hall big enough for services,
and two acres of ground for garden and extension.

They agreed to live in the style of the primitive Christians at Jerusalem, having all things in common and to be regarded as one family. All earnings were to go into the common stock, and there was to be a common table. Each was to have a small allowance, very small, for pocket money ; all were to be considered on an equality, and they were to take turns at the various tasks of the household, the responsibility for domestic arrangements, conducting family worship, and such matters. Thus Carey's ideal was brought into practice, and his own habits of self-denial and frugality became thenceforward the standard of living at Serampore.

The funds brought out being more than expended, an urgent request was sent home for further help until they could get their new plans into operation. These included the opening of a boarding-school for European children by Marshman and the setting up of the press and its development by Ward. Carey, assisted by Fountain, threw himself into the work of preaching in Serampore and the neighbourhood. In the ample grounds surrounding the new property he commenced his botanical garden, the fame of which was destined to be world-wide. Mahogany trees were planted around the houses and soon began to give welcome shade, while the native gardeners, under his directions, transformed the place into a delightful addition to the settlement.

With such alacrity did all get to work that on the 18th of March, barely two months after Carey's arrival at Serampore, Ward placed in his hands the first sheet of the Bengali New Testament. We can imagine the exuberance of joy of the whole party as they handled this treasure, more precious in their estimation than gold. A vista of wondrous possibilities seemed to open before them, and they felt that the evangelisation of India had now indeed begun.

In May Mr. and Mrs. Marshman opened their boarding-school, and very soon were bringing in an income equal to £360 a year. A school was opened, too, for native youths, in which an attendance of forty was registered.

For the future conduct of the Mission an agreement was drawn up, embodying the principles of communistic living that Carey had introduced, and regulating their conduct and affairs with such administrative perfectness that it lasted for seventeen years without any difficulties arising, so long as Fuller and Sutcliff lived to hold the ropes at home. According to the document, they were to cherish an "awful sense of the value of souls"; they were to make "Christ the staple of all their preaching; it is His love alone that can win, and there is no hope but in a ministry of love." The spirit of devotion throughout the agreement is very marked and beautiful. "Finally," they said, "let us give ourselves up unreservedly to this glorious cause. Let us never think that our time, our spirit, our strength, our families, or even the clothes we wear, are our own. Let us sanctify all to God and His cause. Let us for ever shut out the idea of laying up a cowry for ourselves or our children."

At a special thanksgiving meeting held in April they prepared an address of thanks to the Danish king, and in due course he graciously sent them a warm reply, signifying his gratification at the establishing of their Mission in his dominions, and reaffirming the special protection they might expect at his hands.

CHAPTER X.

FIRST-FRUITS.

"The prospects? They are as bright as the promises of God."

JUDSON.

CAREY'S highest ambitions were now being realised. Blessed with the association of fellow-labourers as keen as himself, in a sphere untrammelled by Government restrictions, able to devote his whole time to the work he loved, life was like a song to him. The only drop that was lacking in his cup was the presence of converts—Indian brethren and sisters who might share with them in the labours and pleasures of Christian enterprise.

Ram Bosu, the intellectual pundit, who had left them for a time, came to Serampore in the June of this year. He had a clearer perception of the truths of Christianity than any other Indian of the period, and entertained a philosophical contempt for the popular superstitions, but he could not bring himself to renounce his lifelong associations and avow himself a Christian. It was by no means easy to take such a step, and more especially to be the first to take it. "All the ties," wrote Marshman, "that twine about the heart of a father, a husband, a child, and a neighbour, must be torn and broken before a man can give himself to Christ."

Ram Bosu had even gone to the length of writing

in his cultured Bengali, at the suggestion of Carey,
two tracts, one introducing the doctrines of Christianity
to his countrymen, and the other exposing, with a
remarkable power of sarcasm, the absurdities of
Hinduism. But he was a typical Bengali, the most
sensitive and emotional of Indians. With all his
receptive qualities, his love of novelty and his readiness
to learn, his gift of eloquence and luxuriant imagination, he still shrank from the step that would draw
down on him ostracism and persecution. Hopes of
him, so long indulged, were doomed to end in disappointment, and the honour of leading the van was
reserved for another.

In October, Mr. Thomas, then on a visit to Serampore, was called to set the broken arm of a carpenter,
Krishnu Pal by name. Thomas tied the man to a
tree and set the wounded limb, meanwhile conversing with him with his usual fervour. Strange as the
circumstances may appear to us, the carpenter was
deeply affected, and he became a constant visitor at
the Mission House, receiving the instruction given
with great eagerness. He had been for sixteen years
a guru in a small dissenting sect of Hinduism, and
apparently was peculiarly ready for the news of the
gospel. His wife and daughter often accompanied
him, and the word touched their hearts also. Their
ignorance was great, but never had the missionaries
found people so ready to yield to Christ. The cost
weighed nothing with them, and very soon, to the joy
of the missionaries, Krishnu Pal was urgent in his
request for baptism.

Nor was he alone. Gokul, a Sudra of low caste,
who had traversed the land for years in search of
peace, heard one day the preaching in the Serampore

market-place. Angered by the new religion, he spent the following night in conversation with a friend, eager to show him the absurdity of what he had heard. In spite of his anger he was drawn back to the preachers by the power of an unseen Hand; his sinfulness was laid bare, and his burden increased until he sought rest in Christ. His wife, Joymuni, an earnest woman, came with him, having heard the gospel from her husband's lips.

A love-feast was arranged to be held on the 22nd December, when the two men, Krishnu and Gokul, sat down to eat with the Serampore family. The servants were amazed to see this direct breaking of caste, and from them the news spread through the town like wildfire. A crowd of many hundreds collected, and with fierce imprecations dragged Krishnu and Gokul before the Danish magistrate. As they had no charge to prefer against the two men, the magistrate ordered them to disperse. After considerable threatening the crowd melted away, but some of Krishnu's relatives determined to disguise themselves as robbers and to murder Krishnu and Gokul that night to avenge the insult to their caste. This further violence was only prevented by a sepoy guard placed all night before Krishnu's house.

The courage of Gokul and the women seems to have failed them, but Krishnu, nothing dismayed by the outbreak of popular feeling, was baptized six days later at the same time as Carey's eldest son, Felix. After a preliminary service Carey marched down to the river, with his son on the one side and Krishnu on the other, and followed by the remainder of the missionary band. At the river the governor and many residents had gathered to witness the unique scene, and a dense crowd of Hindus and Mohammedans were also at the spot. Carey explained the rite, and the two candidates were baptized, the European and the Indian, amid perfect order and silence. The service produced a deep impression; the good governor was moved to tears, and even the heathen onlookers seemed to recognise the solemnity of the ceremony. It was remarkable that the first Indian to openly acknowledge as his Saviour the Man of Galilee, who had once been a carpenter, was himself a carpenter.[1]

It was a day of great joy in the Serampore settlement; but to Mr. Thomas, whose hopes had been raised a dozen times to the highest pitch over successive inquirers only to be followed by disappointment in every case, the excitement had proved too much. He had become frantic with joy on the evening when the two men had broken caste, and soon after began to show signs of insanity. Within three days it became necessary to place him under bodily restraint, and when the happy company wended their way to the riverside, Thomas's raving mingled with the cries of poor Mrs. Carey, who was confined in another part of the building.

Other baptisms soon followed. Ignatius Fernandez, a gentleman of Portuguese extraction and independent means, was one of the first. For more than thirty years he continued with the Mission as a most active and successful coadjutor, and was instrumental in raising up a large native church in Dinagepore. Krishnu Pal's sister-in-law was baptized at the same

---

[1] One hundred and twelve years after this event, at the historic spot where Krishnu Pal was baptized, Bishop Azariah, the first Indian bishop, baptized two Indian students. This was his first administration of the rite since consecration to the episcopal office.

A BENGALI BIBLEWOMAN.

Photo by permission]   *[Lee Memorial Mission, Calcutta.*

time. Gokul and his family and Krishnu's wife, Rasu, followed during 1801. Of these Marshman wrote: "There are now six baptized (Indians), whom we esteem more precious than an equal number of gems. We need great prudence in our intercourse with them. We are obliged to strengthen, to encourage, to counteract, to advise, to disapprove, to teach, and yet to do all so as to endear the Saviour to them, and to retain a place in their warmest affections."

The converts were all of comparatively low caste until Petumber Sing joined the number. He was an old man, of great intelligence, and of the Kayust or writer caste—inferior only to the Brahmans. A veritable seeker after truth, he had tried every sect of Hinduism that offered help. Disgusted with his attempts, he had quietly renounced idol-worship, and at an opportune moment one of the Serampore tracts fell into his hands. Without delay he sought out the strangers, and in a few days he openly avowed himself a Christian. A few weeks later two more Kayusts and a Brahman came forward as converts.

On this occasion Carey wrote: "Both Europeans and natives laughed at what they thought our enthusiastic idea of breaking the bonds of Hindu caste by preaching the gospel. When Krishnu and Gokul rejected their caste, many wondered at it; but the majority endeavoured to carry it off with a high hand, and tauntingly asked, 'Have any of the Brahmans or Kayusts believed on Him? What great thing to have a carpenter and a distiller reject their caste?' Lately, however, the Lord has deprived them of that small consolation."

The lowest castes soon had a representative in

Bharut—an old man who said he went to Christ because he was just falling into hell and saw no other way of safety. Peroo, who followed him, was a Mohammedan, and thus the young Church was recruited from all kinds and sections of the community.

The converts displayed a most earnest spirit, and their grasp of Christian truth was very satisfactory. Three of them became successful preachers and teachers. The task before the missionaries was a great one, however, for they were creating not only a new society but a new community. The age-long prejudice of caste and custom did not die easily, but from the beginning a policy was adopted that has been the keystone of all subsequent successful work in India. No concession was made to the demands of caste, and Krishnu Prasad, at his baptism, trod upon his sacred thread, the outward emblem of Brahmanical superiority. Ward, to whom the thread was given, remarked: "This is a more precious relic than any the Church of Rome can boast of." Krishnu, the Brahman, at the celebration of the Supper, received the cup from the hands of Krishnu the Sudra. At the same time the greatest care was taken to avoid all unnecessary interference with the native habits and customs.

Shortly afterwards the first marriage was solemnised between Krishnu Prasad and Onunda, the daughter of Krishnu Pal. The wedding took place under a tree in front of the house. Such a sight had never been seen in Bengal through the whole of its history—a Brahman married to a Sudra in the Christian fashion, and at the wedding supper, Europeans eating with Indians in their own native house at the same table!

Gokul was the first of the Indian Christians to die,

and he passed away rejoicing in his Saviour. This gave the opportunity for a still deeper blow to the bondage of caste. Among the European population the last offices for the dead were carried out by Portuguese pobrees, men of the lowest class, who were often drunk and disorderly. This was not to be the case in the new Christian society. The coffin, made on the Mission premises, was covered with white muslin by Krishnu, at his own expense; and it was carried to the grave on the shoulders of Marshman, Felix Carey, Bhyrub, a converted Brahman, and Peroo, the converted Mohammedan.

As the procession wended its way to the grave, singing as they went the Bengali hymn, "Salvation through the death of Christ," a large crowd of several hundreds of people gazed in astonishment at the strange sight. Great was the impression made by the evident regard and love that Christians manifested towards each other even in death.

CHAPTER XI.

SERAMPORE AT ITS STRENGTH.

"Always abounding in the work of the Lord, forasmuch as ye know that your labour is not in vain in the Lord."

CAREY'S wide experiences at Mudnabatty stood him now in good stead, and he laid his plans with splendid statesmanship. Remarkable success was seen in every department of the work. His zeal was equalled and yet tempered by that of his new comrades, whose ardent devotion was a source of continual strength and joy to him, and to these qualities they united the gift of administrative ability with a large knowledge of the ways of the world.

Serampore proved a good centre for evangelistic work because of the vast crowds that came there to worship. Carey tells of a million people meeting "for the purpose of bathing a wooden idol, near Serampore, whose name is Juggernaut, which signifies, 'The Lord of the World.'"

Attended by one or another of the company, Carey spent much time in preaching at the street corners or in the villages in the neighbourhood. His spirit was greatly stirred by the state of the people. "This country is very populous and as full of idolatry as it can hold," he wrote, and goes on to show his distress at the open immorality. There often seemed no conscience to appeal to in those that listened. The

gatherings were sometimes noisy; but when the sufferings and love of Christ were touched upon, the people
were all attention. Hours were spent in discussions
with those around, when unlimited patience had to be
shown with questionings that would seem like quibbles
to those unacquainted with the Hindu mind.

On one occasion a Brahman who had been listening
urged that Carey should believe on Krishnu and be
saved. The little missionary placed himself at the
side of the Brahman, and said, "'Well, appoint me a
day to invest me with the Poitoo (the sacred thread of
the Brahmans), and teach me the Gayotee (the verse
taught at investment). 'Oh,' says he, 'you cannot
become a Brahman; you must be a Sudra.' 'Yes,'
says I, 'a pretty business! You want to put me under
your feet, do you? Is this your religion and benevo-
lence? I preach the gospel to you that you may
become my brother, my beloved friend; and you invite
me to embrace your Shastras that I may become your
slave!'"

Ward and Marshman were soon able to join in the
preaching, for they both displayed similar linguistic
ability to that for which Carey was distinguished.
Ward, indeed, acquired a grasp of the colloquial that
neither Carey nor Marshman attained to, and seldom
has any foreigner been as able as he to rivet the
attention of a native audience by the easy idiom and
humour of his address. He was able to go alone and
preach in Bengali before he was in the country a year,
and that in spite of the incessant work of the press.

From the beginning the plan was formed of training
Indian itinerants who, retaining all the simplicity of
native habits, would command ready access to the
hearts of their fellow-countrymen to whom they could

THE CAR OF JUGGERNAUT.

appeal in their own mother-tongue. The first converts were therefore pressed into the service of the gospel, and throughout its whole history the Serampore Mission has kept this prominently before the Indian Church. The great work grew out of the narrowest resources, and it is as we recognise the smallness of these that we are able to appreciate the tremendous faith called for from these early men. Their first preachers, Eurasian and Indian, were men who had no training for their work, and if that work was thorough and successful the credit lies with the leaders who inspired them.

Ward's printing press was a power for good. Tracts and leaflets were prepared in great numbers and scattered over the country. Even as early as 1800 it was possible to say, " The natives received our printed papers and books with the greatest eagerness, and they . . . are extensively read. One man says he has lent his book to a friend at a distance; another meets us and repeats what he has found in a hymn, perhaps; another attempts to find fault with what he has read."

But the energies of the printers were chiefly directed to the completion of the Bengali New Testament. Lack of competent assistance made it necessary for Ward to set up almost the whole of the type with his own hands. It was an enormous task, but with such perseverance was it carried out that the volume was ready for use by February 1801. The day that Carey had dreamed of for years had at last arrived; there was now nothing lacking for the conquest of the land for Christ. Every man around could have the words of God in his own tongue.

The mass of the people, however, could not read, for they had no means of learning, and this problem engaged the attention of the missionaries. Marshman's central school for Hindus was flourishing because there the scholars might learn English, a knowledge of which was fast becoming an asset in commercial life. But there seemed no general sense of the need of education; its advantages were not apparent, and for years to come Carey's idea of a wide system of primary schools progressed but slowly.

Meanwhile, the little missionary force was sadly depleted. Fountain was taken from them in the midst of their early labours of the first year at Serampore. He had gone on a visit to Dinagepore and died there on the 20th of August. The next year, during the rains, Brunsdon followed him at the early age of twenty-four, having shown a spirit of great devotion to his work. Three months later Thomas died, after a painful illness, at Dinagepore, and was buried alongside Fountain. His career had been by no means a shining example, but he was possessed of many noble qualities that went far to redeem his conspicuous failings. The two graves bear no names to-day; they are but shapeless mounds overgrown with wild vegetation; but the men were of the pioneers in that vast land, and sealed their testimony with their lives.

Thus in two years the missionary force was reduced to three men. But fresh recruits were already on their way from England. Chamberlain, destined to be of great power among Europeans, was the first to arrive, and four more followed—the early promise of that great stream of men and women which has flowed steadily into India through the century. With the coming of reinforcements the policy of the work developed, and out-stations were speedily opened. Leave for these had been unsuccessfully sought from the British Government time and again, until the missionaries decided to await permission no longer. Carey's two eldest sons, Felix and William, were giving evidence of usefulness, and besides the new arrivals from England there were men converted in the country, Eurasian and Indian, and for so many Serampore was too small a field. The first out-station to be opened was Kutwa.

Seven years after the removal to Serampore Mrs. Carey died, having been under continual restraint for twelve years.

In 1802 the Rev. David Brown retired from his long service in Calcutta, and took up his residence at Aldeen, on the banks of the river at Serampore. His home became a resort for the choicer spirits of evangelical Anglicanism, and brought many into touch with the Serampore Mission.

Among these was the saintly chaplain, Henry Martyn. At the extremity of Aldeen grounds there stood an old temple, small, but with massive walls, from which the image had been removed owing to the encroachment of the river. This now belonged to Mr. Brown, and was used as a meeting-place where churchmen and dissenters met together for prayer. It came to be known as Martyn's Pagoda, since he occupied it during his stay at Serampore. He thus described it :—

"My habitation assigned me by Mr. Brown is a pagoda in his grounds, on the edge of the river. Thither I retired at night, and really felt something like superstitious dread at being in a place once inhabited, as it were, by devils, but yet felt disposed to be triumphantly joyful that the temple where they were worshipped was become Christ's oratory. I

prayed out aloud to my God, and the echoes returned
from the vaulted roof. Oh, may I so pray that the
dome of heaven may resound! I like my dwelling
much, it is so retired and free from noise; it has so
many recesses that I can hardly find my way in
and out."

To this retired spot came Carey and his friends

MARTYN'S PAGODA.

Photo by]   *[L. Bevan Jones.*

frequently, especially during Martyn's long visit, and
in the strange oratory, with its intricate recesses, while
Martyn's organ dispensed sweet music, they blended
their praises with those of one so thoroughly congenial.
Carey says of those occasions: "As the shadow of
bigotry is not known among us here, we take sweet
counsel together, and go to the house of God as friends."
By Martyn the intercourse was equally prized, for he
wrote: "Three such men as Carey, Marshman, and

Ward, so united to one another and to their work, are not to be found, I should think, in the whole world."

Those were days when there were giants in the land, for not only were there meetings of men so renowned in Christian fame as Carey, Marshman, Ward, and Martyn, but others also of fragrant memory were more or less closely associated with early Serampore. Thither came Adoniram Judson to receive blessing and help on his way to Burma. Bishop Heber found congenial companions in the Mission, and Havelock, the great soldier, had a deep spiritual experience in their little chapel. Duff frequently came to them, many years later, while Lords Wellesley and Hastings, two of India's most enlightened rulers, thought it not lowering to their dignity to confer with the three brethren on matters that affected the well-being of the land.

In the midst of busy work and happy associations, the growing family at Serampore maintained its primitive simplicity. They dined together at long tables (Martyn speaks of one hundred and fifty sitting down to a meal), missionaries, wives, children, and scholars. "We live moderately," one of them wrote. "We have always a little cheap fruit, goat's flesh, broth, fowls, with a little beef sometimes, and curry, and we have good wheaten bread."

Writing in 1815, Marshman said: "No missionary here has a single servant about him; every article of food and clothing for himself and his whole family is covered by sixty rupees a month, and there is no conveyance at the Mission House in spite of the number of females and the extreme heat of the climate."

Pervading all there was a beautiful spirit of contentment and fervent piety. Prayer, individual and united, characterised the whole establishment.

It is to be remembered that this strict economy was practised without a thought of change, even when the missionaries were bringing in large sums to the common purse. Carey, as will be seen later, was, from 1800, earning £700 a year as professor of languages in Calcutta, a sum subsequently increased to £1200 and ultimately to £1800. Marshman's school, which, under the able management of himself and his wife, was the most flourishing and remunerative in the country, earned £1000 a year for many years; while Ward's printing brought in no inconsiderable sum. They had been expected, as had their predecessors in South India, to find their own support, and this they did with hearty goodwill.

What was unique in the Serampore men was the novel resolution they voluntarily adopted of consecrating the whole of their income to the cause they had embarked upon. Previous missionaries had become moderately rich; *these* lived and died poor. Carey and Marshman, with their families, accepted only £40 a year for their private expenses, while Ward, unmarried, managed on £20. Ten pounds extra, as a special grant, was given to Carey to enable him to appear in decent clothes in Calcutta.

Even Mr. Fuller considered that they carried the principle of self-denial too far, and proposed that they should keep a proportion of all their earnings for themselves. This, for many years, they positively refused to do, replying that having given themselves and their families to the Mission, should they hold back any profit of their labours from Him to whom they owed everything!

In 1817, however, acting on the repeated advice of Mr. Fuller, they decided to devote a tithe of all their private income to making provision for their families in case of their own death. Two years later, when forced by calumnies in England to make an examination of their affairs, they found that during the twenty years of their life in Serampore they had devoted to the Mission altogether the sum of almost £50,000,—the entire surplus of their earnings after deducting the meagre amount of their personal expenses.

The little group of converts had grown rapidly. By 1809 there were 200 in church membership, including Europeans, and that year there were 60 more baptized, 27 of whom were English soldiers. Out-station work had increased, and they were able to record the founding of five churches in Bengal and one in Burma.

Six years later, in the last letter transmitted to Fuller before his death, a review of the work is made. It told of six stations in Bengal with resident missionaries, and four more occupied by native brethren; four in the Upper Provinces, one in Surat, and one each in Amboyna, Burma, and Ceylon. These were occupied by nine missionaries from England, fifteen European and East Indians engaged in the country, and twenty-seven native preachers. Seven hundred and sixty-five baptisms had taken place, of which more than 500 were of Indians. The New Testament was printed or in the press, in whole or in part, in a dozen languages of India, and grammars had been published in several of these. Hundreds of thousands of tracts had been circulated. Of schools there were more than a score for Indian children, besides Marshman's English seminary. The first Sunday school, started in 1803 by Carey's sons at Serampore, was the tiny beginning of a great movement, destined yet to be one of the most potent influences in the evangelisation of the land.[1]

It was frankly acknowledged that the missionaries taken on in the country were defective in some of the qualifications for the work, the native preachers lacked training, and the translations were imperfect. But when every deduction is made, the fact of a great and wonderful success will remain. The pioneers had to plant their gospel in a land where all was against them, and where everything had to be created, even to the very grammars necessary for the acquirement of the language. A Christian society representing more than 2000 persons had been gathered out from among the heathen. Ignorance, self-conceit, timidity, indolence, and perverseness had to be prayed and wept over and rebuked; but, to the joy of the missionaries, the majority of the converts lived to adorn the gospel. The day of grace had begun in Bengal.

[1] In 1913, the Sunday-school scholars of India numbered nearly 700,000, with a fast-increasing army of 30,000 teachers.

CHAPTER XII.

THE PROFESSOR.

"So, as much as in me is I am ready to preach the gospel to you that are at Rome also."

LORD WELLESLEY was one of the ablest rulers Britain has sent to India. On his arrival in that land as Governor-General in 1798, he discovered that many who were in high positions of authority had so small an acquaintance with the language and customs of the people that they were unfitted for the tasks that fell to them. The days were past when the Company's officials were simply traders; they were in reality ministers and servants of the King of England, and their positions carried with them heavy responsibility. Cadets were appointed at as early an age as fifteen years, and their education needed completion, especially in the matter of Oriental languages.

For this purpose Fort William College was established in Calcutta in 1800, and there the junior servants of the Company were required to continue their studies for three years. The Rev. David Brown was appointed as Provost, and the Rev. Claudius Buchanan as Vice-Provost. William Carey was the only man then in the country who was thoroughly qualified to teach Bengali, and he was invited to accept the position of Professor of that language.

A difficulty arose over his Nonconformist principles

which made it impossible for him to pass the religious test instituted at the instance of Buchanan; but this was overcome by giving him a lower grade than a professorship with a salary of £600 a year—considerably less than he was entitled to for the post he was now to occupy. Being a missionary, he was not acceptable to the permanent officials at Calcutta; but Wellesley made the appointment after merely satisfying himself concerning Carey's reputation and ability. With characteristic sturdiness, Carey demanded and was granted full freedom of action as a missionary, in spite of the fact that missionaries were under the ban of the Company.

The new appointment brought Carey into a position of considerable influence, which was of the greatest assistance to the young Mission. He immediately threw his weight into the movement that was making for the purifying of the tone of Calcutta society; and his learning attracted to him many friends from among both the foreign and the native community. He remained the most notable figure in the College throughout its history. His Calcutta study was the centre of incessant literary work as his Serampore study was the centre of Bible translation. He spent four days a week in Calcutta and three in Serampore, and employed three pundits daily at each.

Of the hundred original volumes in Oriental languages sent out from Fort William College, he contributed the lion's share. At the opening of the College not a single prose work existed in the Bengali language. He employed the talents of Ram Bosu in compiling a history of a Hindu king, and thus began the ever-increasing output of Bengali books which to-day pours forth in a vast stream from Indian presses.

Assisted by Marshman, and under Government auspices, he undertook the publication of some of the most celebrated Sanskrit works, beginning with the Ramayana. Already overworked, they contented themselves with the fact that this additional labour would provide the means for the opening of one more station in the Mission.

The men destined to be leaders throughout India sat at Carey's feet and learnt not only to master the languages of the people they were to rule, but to treat the natives kindly, and not a few came to love them as brethren. It was the influence of Fort William College that, more than aught else, gave to the East Indian Services those high ideals of integrity and ability that have rendered it of world-wide fame down to our own day

Honours flowed in on Carey as the years passed. His subject in the College was extended so as to include Sanskrit and Mahratti, and he was ultimately granted the full title of Professor of Oriental Languages, with a largely augmented salary. "This," he said, "will much help the Mission."

A brilliant speech made by him both in Bengali and Sanskrit at one of the annual disputations of the College in the presence of the Governor-General and a large number of leading Europeans and Indians brought him great renown. This, the first address ever delivered in Sanskrit by a European, was translated and published by order of Lord Wellesley, who expressed himself as highly delighted with it. He went on to say concerning that part of the address which made mention of his own enlightened policy: "I esteem such a testimony from such a man a greater honour than the applause of courts and parliaments."

From the standpoint of missions, the immediate gain was that before the chief representative of British government Carey had frankly avowed himself as a missionary without being called to account.

In 1807 the Faculty of the Brown University in the United States conferred upon him the degree of Doctor of Divinity in recognition of his unique service to the Church of God. Later the King of Denmark wrote to the Serampore Mission expressing his deep interest in the work they were doing, and desiring to decorate Dr. Carey with an order. This was respectfully declined, but in a subsequent communication the kindly sovereign begged them to accept a gold medal at his hands and the title-deeds of a large house in a very eligible part of Serampore.

It was no wonder that, even with Carey's earlier honours, Fuller and the men at home grew fearful of danger in the applause and patronage of the great. But no man was ever less affected by popularity than Carey.

From the days of his arrival at the College, Carey had sought to start work among the large population of the Indian metropolis. The needs of the neglected European and Eurasian poor had appealed to him from the days of his first residence in Calcutta, and he commenced now to hold services for them in the house of a kindly-disposed undertaker. The worshippers had to enter amid rows of coffins and funereal trappings, a state of things that Carey yearned to change by the erection of an undenominational chapel.

There were difficulties in the way of more direct missionary effort, especially among Bengalis, and great care had to be exercised because of the intense opposition on the part of the Government. It was

1806 before a centre for work was obtained. A site was secured in the Bow Bazaar, a crowded thoróughfare, and the liquor shops and houses of ill-fame that had hitherto held the ground were quickly pulled down.[1] A temporary thatched house was erected, and on Sunday the 1st of June it was opened by Mr. Ward with divine service.

This was the first time that the gospel had been preached to the inhabitants of Calcutta in their own tongue. It was the end of the long hot season, and although the city was aflame with the brilliant red flowers of the gold mohur trees, all life was at a low ebb. And yet crowds streamed in to hear a European gentleman preaching in Bengali. Mr. Ward and the native preachers were followed down the street by an excited crowd which poured abuse on them.

Two Sundays later the appearance of a converted Brahman in the pulpit created great astonishment, and the news spread all over the neighbourhood. The Government officials were besieged with importunate demands from the Hindus, and an order was given whereby preaching in the vernacular was absolutely prohibited.

It was a wonderful sight—the Hackleton cobbler spending his days in training the governing class of India in Oriental languages and translating the great epics of Hinduism, and when the sun had set, returning to the society of the poor, maimed, halt, and blind, to preach in their own tongues the glad tidings of a Saviour for the heathen of Europe and Asia alike. So great was the willingness to listen to them that the

---

[1] "The inhabitants thereabouts may emphatically be called SINNERS," recorded Mr. Ward, for it was a hotbed of immorality, the haunt of sailors who disgraced their European name by every excess.

preachers would find themselves wedged in a large crowd which would stand for hours together listening.

Carey found it necessary to give one evening a week to seeing inquirers, and of this he wrote: "The number of inquirers constantly coming forward, awakened by the instrumentality of the brethren, fills me with joy. . . . . Seldom fewer than twenty come (weekly), and the simple confessions of their sinful state . . . the expressions of trust in Christ . . . often attended with tears which almost choke their utterance, present a scene of which you can scarcely entertain an adequate idea."

In many other directions Carey found opportunities for doing good. By his untiring efforts a school for poor Eurasian children on undenominational lines was opened, and he and Marshman fostered this institution until it was strongly established and their assistance could be safely withdrawn. He joined with Lord Hastings, the successor to Wellesley, in starting the Calcutta School Book Society to supply the wants of material for the schools springing up on all sides; and he was able to encourage the spread of education by urging upon the Government its duty in this direction. He initiated the Agricultural Society of Calcutta for developing the resources of the country, and by his energy and spirit this society eventually embraced hundreds of members in every province, and was of the widest service.

Largely through his influence, the practice of sacrificing children at the mouth of the Ganges was brought to the direct notice of the Government. To him was given the acceptable commission by the Governor-General of consulting the ancient authorities adduced by Hindus for this terrible custom; and after examination he reported that it was not sanctioned by the Hindu Shastras, and ought to be put down. An enact-ment was accordingly passed absolutely prohibiting the practice under the severest penalties, and it ceased from that day.

He laboured hard at the same time to have the custom of suttee suppressed; but Lord Wellesley, owing to his near departure from India, felt that he could not deal with so great a matter. The missionary did not waver in his purpose, however, and he had his reward in 1829 when Lord William Bentinck declared by regulation the practice of suttee criminal and all abetters of the deed to be deemed guilty of homicide.

The regulation was sent to Carey to be translated into Bengali, and the order reached him on Sunday morning as he was preparing for service. Throwing off his black coat, he exclaimed, "No church for me to-day. If I delay an hour to translate and publish this, many a widow's life may be sacrificed." Leaving the pulpit to be occupied by another, he completed the translation before night.

Carey's life in Calcutta was extraordinarily full. Every Monday evening at sunset he left Serampore in his boat and was rowed down the eighteen miles of winding river, working at his books all the way. When the busy four days' work in the metropolis was through, the early tide bore him swiftly up the Hooghly again to the study where he gave himself once more to his translations.

From a letter in which he apologises for delay in writing we may see how the days in Calcutta were occupied: "I rose this morning at a quarter before six, read a chapter in the Hebrew Bible, and spent the time till seven in private addresses to God, and then attended family prayer with the servants in Bengali. While tea was getting ready I read a little Persian with a moonshi who was waiting when I left my bedroom; and also before breakfast a portion of the Scriptures in Hindustani. The moment breakfast was over, sat down to the translation of the Ramayana from Sanskrit with a pundit, who was also waiting, and continued this translation till ten, at which hour I went to College and attended the duties there till between one and two o'clock.

"When I returned home I examined a proof sheet of the Bengali translation of Jeremiah, which took till dinner-time. . . . After dinner, translated, with the assistance of the chief pundit of the College, the greater part of the eighth chapter of Matthew into Sanskrit. This employed me till six. After six sat down with a Telinga pundit to learn that language. At seven I began to collect a few previous thoughts into the form of a sermon, and preached at half-past seven. About forty persons were present, among them one of the puisne judges. . . . Afterwards I got a subscription from him of 500 rupees towards erecting our new place of worship. . . . Preaching was over and the congregation gone by nine. I then sat down and translated the eleventh of Ezekiel into Bengali, and this lasted till near eleven, and now I sit down to write to you."

This needs no comment, but we can well understand the significance of an allusion in a letter sent home to the Committee in 1817, wherein Carey is referred to as "our aged brother," though he was then only fifty-six.

CHAPTER XIII.

THE FIGHT WITH THE COMPANY.

"The rulers take counsel together against the Lord. . . . He that sitteth in the heavens shall laugh."

THE East India Company, which had attempted with unwearying determination to prevent the evangelisation of India, now found it impossible to confine the gospel to Danish Serampore. The printed page carried the message far and wide; converts became evangelists, and mission stations were opened, wherever possible, close to the borders of British territory.

But this was not all. In the irony of fate, the Company had unwittingly become an important confederate in the dissemination of the gospel. By appointing Carey to Fort William College, it supplied him for many years with the means for carrying on the work, and by his intercourse with pundits of many nations it gave him not only the opportunity of scattering the good seed over a wide area, but of enlisting the finest linguistic talent available in India in the task of translating the Scriptures.

Days of storm, however, were fast approaching. The animosity of the Calcutta secretaries, men "cradled in despotism and nursed in prejudice," restrained during Lord Wellesley's tenure of office, found its chance with the arrival of Lord Minto. The new Governor-General, though a professed friend of liberty and a man of enlightened views, was weak in character and anxious to please those he had come to rule. News of a terrible massacre of British troops at Vellore met him at Madras, and he was informed that the outbreak was a result of missionary interference with the natives. He was prepared, therefore, to adopt stringent measures for the suppression of the Serampore Mission when this course was urged upon him by his subordinates.

An excuse was soon found. An unfortunate translation of a Persian tract, printed at Serampore, and containing irritating strictures on Mohammed, was reported to him as a grave matter. Spies were sent by the Government to attend the missionaries' meetings, and in the guise of inquirers to get copies of all the pamphlets they could find. One of the informers reported that an elderly native had descanted in a meeting on the shortcomings of the Brahmans, had said that they could not forgive sins, and that Hindu festivals tended to increase rather than lessen transgression!

As a result of this, the Governor wrote a strong letter to the Serampore missionaries demanding the immediate closing of the Calcutta chapel and the cessation of all publications that aimed at the conversion of the natives. Open-air preaching was to be discontinued, and the press to be brought immediately to Calcutta. A similar letter was sent to the Danish Governor. The exultation of the anti-missionary party was great, for they felt that a death-blow had now been given to the enterprise.

The missionaries met in dismay. The demand regarding the press was unwarrantable, for it stood in neutral territory; and the argument now urged by

Government that they were pledged to the perpetual exclusion of Christianity was absurd. After prolonged prayer, they met with the Danish Governor and Mr. Brown, who advised them simply to acknowledge the letter and wait. The Governor plainly said that he should not for a moment listen to the demand for extradition made by the Calcutta authorities; rather than that he would strike his flag and leave the country.

The expedient was at length suggested of the missionaries seeing Lord Minto and explaining in person. He received them graciously, and accepted a memorial, drawn up with great care and skill, detailing the aims and the spirit of the Mission. This at once convinced him, and the obnoxious order regarding the press was rescinded a few days later. " The crests of our enemies are fallen," wrote Carey.

A long dispatch was sent to England by the Calcutta Council, explaining the whole affair and advising that no more missionaries be allowed to come to the country, as it was difficult to restrain their zeal. The reply to this was a complete surprise. It was prepared by Dundas, a director, but an earnest Christian gentleman. He said that the missionaries were evidently men of moral rectitude, and it was hoped that in any future difficulties private communication be entered into with them before an order was issued. With regard to new missionaries being permitted to enter the country, he added : " none of the meritorious individuals who devoted themselves to missionary labours had proceeded to Bengal with the Company's licence."

With this the incident ended in India, but a fierce conflict sprang up in England. Enraged at the unexpected attitude of Mr. Dundas, old Anglo-Indians came forward to attack the Mission in a series of defamatory pamphlets. The most extravagant things were written of the missionaries, who "were invading the dearest rights and wounding the tenderest feelings of the natives." One affirmed that "the mind of man had never conceived a wilder or more dangerous plan than that of instituting schools in India." The missionaries were represented as "illiterate, ignorant, and, as enthusiastic (*i.e.* fanatical) as the wildest devotees of the Hindus." The men and women who through their preaching had found peace in Christ and whose lives splendidly attested the regenerating power of God were spoken of with contempt.

Replies were speedily forthcoming to these attacks and Fuller wrote an Apology in three parts. This was widely read, and produced a powerful and favourable effect on the public mind.

The most embittered of the opponents of the Mission at this time was the Rev. Sidney Smith, the renowned satirist, who poured upon Carey in particular the coarsest ridicule.

The discussions closed with an able article by Southey, in which he reviewed the work done by Carey and his associates, and, with fine sarcasm, drew the conclusion that "in fourteen years 'these low-born, low-bred mechanics' (as they had been termed) have done more towards spreading the knowledge of the Scriptures among the heathen than has been accomplished or even attempted by all the world besides."

The storm was lulled for a time, but the missionaries knew that the authorities in Calcutta only awaited a further pretext for opposition. This was the more keenly felt when the same Government was openly encouraging the grossest forms of idolatry. "Last week," wrote Ward, "a deputation from Government went in procession to Kali Ghat—the most opulent and popular shrine in the metropolis—and presented 5000 rupees to the idol in the name of the Company for the success which had attended the British arms." And they had furthermore undertaken to receive the infamous shrine of Juggernaut under their especial protection until peremptorily ordered to desist by the directors in England.

On the arrival of Judson and Newell from America in 1812 the storm broke out with redoubled fury. They were ordered out of India at once, and while the unfortunate recruits were considering the best course of action, the dilemma was increased by the arrival of six more missionaries from England. The most extreme measures were now taken by the authorities, and some of the new-comers suffered the indignity of being haled to the common prison by sepoy guards. Several of them had to leave the country in one direction or another. Lawson, who had come to help Ward in the press, was ordered away as a missionary, but, on the intercession of Marshman, allowed to remain as a punch-cutter.

The Company's charter was almost due for renewal, and Carey urged that an immediate campaign be started in England to secure the insertion of a distinct clause allowing missionaries freedom to enter India. " The fault lies in the clause which gives the Company power to send home interlopers," he wrote, " and is just as reasonable as one which should forbid all the people in England, a select few excepted, to look at the moon. The prohibition is wrong ; and nothing that is morally wrong can be politically right."

The suggestion commended itself to Fuller, and in concert with the leaders of other more recently formed missionary societies he threw himself into the task with his usual energy. They secured the interest of such men as Grant and Dundas on the Board of Directors, and of Wilberforce and the friends of liberty in Parliament. Interviews with the Prime Minister and others in authority proving futile, the zealots traversed the country, addressing public meetings. Denounced by Indian civilians and military men, pursued with a deadly hatred by the Company, opposed by the majority of the House, deceived by the suave words of political leaders, and even deserted by Christian ministers, the small band held right on in their purpose. They appealed to the people, and the people responded ; and once again was God's arm bared in the defence of His cause. Public opinion was roused to such an extent that Parliament was flooded with petitions.

Meanwhile the Anglo-Indians, confident of success, with almost the entire press at their back, prepared to oppose rigorously any alteration in the charter. So great, however, was the popular outcry that the Prime Minister, Lord Castlereagh, himself brought forward, in May 1813, the "Christianising Resolution," as Wilberforce aptly termed it. The mode in which it was introduced revealed Castlereagh's utter indifference. This was followed by long and carefully planned speeches, in which the usual vilifying of the missionaries was gone through. Then Wilberforce rose, and with one of his finest flights of oratory held the House spellbound for the space of three hours. A great impression was made, and the resolution was passed at three in the morning by a majority of eighty-nine to thirty-six.

The third reading of the Bill for the renewal of

the Charter was fixed for the 13th July, and a last great attempt was made by the Anglo-Indians to prevent the introduction of the clause. An eloquent Madras lawyer named Marsh, in an elaborate, brilliant, and ferocious speech, poured his wrath upon the missionaries.

Despite Marsh and his kind, the clause was passed by a final majority of twenty-two. Thus the sanction of Britain was given to the introduction of the gospel to India, after a struggle that will be for ever memorable in the annals of the Christian Church.

The new Governor-General, Lord Moira, about to leave for the East, had been deeply impressed with the noble outburst of enthusiasm that had been displayed. From the date of his arrival in Calcutta the attitude of Government was utterly changed towards Missions, and they began to receive the courteous consideration they so well deserved.

CHAPTER XIV.

WEAPONS OF WAR.

" The especial grace given to Carey was that—as an Eastern Wiclif —he should be the pioneer of Bible translation and Christian literature in India."—CULROSS.

IN the early days, while still engaged at his shoe-making, Carey had hammered out his system of evangelisation. With sanctified genius he had recognised that the main instrument in the great work must be the Bible translated into the vernaculars of the peoples. On the journey out he applied himself diligently to the rudiments of Bengali, and though, having neither native teacher, grammar, nor text-book, his progress was slow, he had before landing made a translation of the first chapter of Genesis!

His first intention had been only to translate the Bible into this vernacular, but he was soon convinced that much more than this was required. While at Mudnabatty he had carried his studies of Sanskrit to such a degree as to be a master in that language, and this widened his ambitions in the matter of translation. The arrival of Marshman and Ward, men with abilities scarcely inferior to his own in this respect, and fully sharing his enthusiasm, had led to the propounding of a great scheme that included the translation of the Bible into all the languages of the East.

They understood that there were seven principal

ଶାବଥ ସ୍କୁଲ ପାଠ ।

ଯୀଶୁର ଜନ୍ମ ।   (୧)

ସାରବାଣୀ । "ସେ ଇଶ୍ୱରରୂପୀ ହୋଇ ଅପଣା କୁ ଇଶ୍ୱର ତୁଲ୍ୟ ମଣି ବାଛୁ ଅପହରଣ ବୋଧ ନ କରି, ଅପଣାକୁ ଶୂନ୍ୟ କରି ମନୁଷ୍ୟ କେସ ଏରୂ ଦାସସ୍ୱରୂପୀ ହେଲେ ।" ଫି ୨; ୬-୭ ।

ପାଠ ।

ଲୂକ ୨; ୧, ୩-୧୦ ।

୧ ଅଉ ସେକ୍ୱାଲରେ ଗୃହ୍ୟର ସମୟ ଲୋକଙ୍କ ନାମ ଲେଖି ଦେବାକୁ ଅଗସ୍ତ କାଇସର ଦ୍ୱାର ଅଜ୍ଞା ପ୍ରଣୁରଢ ହେଲ । ୩ ଏହେତୁ ନାମ ଲେଖାଇବା ନମନ୍ତେ ସମସ୍ତେ ଅପଣା ନଗରକୁ ଗମନ କଲେ । ୪ ଏଥିରେ ଯୁଷଫ ନାମ ଲେଖି ଦେବା ନମନ୍ତେ ଅପଣାର ବାଗ୍‌ଦତ୍ତ ସ୍ତ୍ରୀ ମାର୍ୟ୍ୟାଙ୍କ ସଙ୍ଗେ ସେନ ଗାଲ୍ଲୀ ପ୍ରଦେଶର ନାଜରତ୍ତ ନଗରରୁ ଯିହୂଦୀ ଦେଶର ବେଥ୍‌ଲିହିମ ନାମକ ଦାଉଦର ନଗରକୁ ଗଲ, ୫ ଯେହେତୁ ସେ ଦାଉଦର କୁଲଙ୍କ ଓ ବଂଶଜାତ ଥିଲ; ସେ ସମୟରେ ମାର୍ୟ୍ୟା ଗର୍ବବତୀ ଥଲ । ୬ ସେମ୍ୟାନେ ସେହି ସ୍ଥାନରେ ଥାଉଁଥାଉଁ ମାର୍ୟ୍ୟାର ପ୍ରସବ ସମୟ ସମ୍ପୂର୍ଣ୍ଣ ହେଲେ ସେ ଅପଣା ପ୍ରଥମଜାତ ସନ୍ତାନ ପ୍ରସବ କଲ ।

A PAGE OF NEW TESTAMENT, IN ORIYA.

languages in India, and they urged that at least the New Testament should be put into each of these. They possessed considerable experience, they had the help of learned pundits at Fort William College, and the kindly protection of the Danish Government in their labours. Translations were already commenced in Urdu, Oriya, and Mahratti, besides the completed Bengali Bible. They asked assistance of the Society of £1000 a year, and to this Fuller agreed readily. By a long and arduous tour of preaching he raised £1300, and American help increased this to £2000.

Meanwhile, Serampore had become a busy hive of activity in the matter of printing, and an efficient type-foundry had been established. For this Carey had secured the assistance of a Hindu named Panchanan, who had a natural gift for type-casting, and this man and his disciple continued to do this service for the Mission for nearly half a century, their work being thorough and beautiful. They would only work under their special idol, and remained Hindus to the end, though their labours were used mightily in the extension of the Kingdom. With such assistants, Ward successfully grappled with the task of producing type of every language they needed, though, in the majority of cases, it was work that had never been before attempted.

In 1809 they were able to report a fine edition of the Bengali Bible in five volumes, and a third and improved version of the New Testament in that language. The New Testament and Psalms were published in Oriya, the New Testament in Sanskrit, while Telugu and Panjabi editions were under way and the Gospels were ready in Urdu.

All their ventures were prospering when a terrible calamity overtook them.

At six o'clock one evening in March 1812, a fire broke out in the printing office, and, in spite of all their efforts to extinguish it, it quickly spread to the whole establishment. At midnight, with a terrible crash, the roof fell in, and the imprisoned flames shot up in a great column of fire, steady as that of a vast candle. Within the blazing premises were treasures of value beyond computation—sets of type for fourteen Eastern languages, all wrought with the utmost care; piles of Scriptures ready for distribution; hundreds of reams of paper; and, most valuable of all, manuscripts which no money could replace. Carey was in Calcutta at the time, and news of the disaster was carried to him by Marshman. He was so stunned by the blow that for a while he could not utter a word.

But they were not the kind of men to lose time in lamentations, and even as they arrived back at Serampore they found Ward already busily gathering from the ruins whatever remained of type-punches and moulds. An empty warehouse of their own was utilised as a new office, and type-casters were set to work at once. With such indomitable energy did they all labour, that in six weeks five new founts of type were made, and printing was hurrying on in all these languages; and within two months of hearing of the disaster, Fuller was circulating amongst subscribers pieces of the version made from the new type, inscribed with the words, "feathers of the phoenix."

Little did the plodding scholars think that this fire was to be used by the Master in making their work famous all over Europe and America, and to call forth wider sympathy and worthier support than they had ever yet known. But so it was. From Calcutta came the first help, a sum of £800, collected within a few days; and when the news reached England, the sympathy evoked there was so real that the whole of the pecuniary loss was made up in less than three months.

In 1821 we hear of nineteen presses all hard at work, and two years later a *Memoir of Translations* tells of Bibles, or portions, in twenty languages. Some of these were large and important languages, while others, we know to-day, were but provincial dialects. The *Memoir* was accompanied by a map of India, defining by a distinct colour the area over which each language was used. Their scheme, formulated seventeen years before was now as nearly complete as lay within the powers of even such giants as these to make it. And yet there were more wonders to follow; for by the end of another ten years the Bible, in whole or in part, had been translated at Serampore into the incredible number of thirty-six languages.

Of all these perhaps the most remarkable translation was that into Chinese, a language taken up as a recreation by Ward and Marshman! Ward commenced the study in 1806 almost without facilities of any kind, and devoted to it for fifteen years all the leisure he could create by encroaching upon his hours of sleep.

Marshman joined him in the study, and carried the task farther on by completing the Old Testament, and in 1823 he had the joy of presenting the British and Foreign Bible Society with a finished copy. The whole of this translation had to be printed from wooden blocks and not from moveable type; twelve men were kept constantly at work upon it.

Behind the task of Bible translation lay a great deal that might easily miss due recognition. For in all these languages, grammars and dictionaries had to be prepared before the greater work could be even begun; and in this matter alone the labours of Carey and his associates were incalculable. Carey himself produced dictionaries and grammars in more than a dozen languages, and the labour involved in these may be estimated by a description given by himself of one of the largest of them: "I am now printing a dictionary of the Bengali, which will be pretty large, for I have got to page 256 quarto, and am not through the first letter." We naturally wonder how many quarto pages there were when the dictionary was finished; and we remember Samuel Johnson's sympathetic definition of a lexicographer—"a harmless drudge!"

Tracts in great quantities and in a large variety of languages were poured out from the press and scattered far and wide. Books, too, of general interest were not thought to be outside their scope. Hindu and Sanskrit epics and histories were produced, chiefly at the desire of Government, and Ward brought out a valuable work on the *History, Mythology, and Literature of the Hindus*. A Christian newspaper that held its own for nearly three-quarters of a century was started and carried on with increasing usefulness. Marshman produced as early as 1810 an English translation of the *Works of Confucius*, and three years later his *Key to the Chinese Language* so pleased the Government of Calcutta that they voted him £1000 from the public purse towards the expense of publication.

The mere recital of these prodigious labours fills us with amazement.

CHAPTER XV.

THE HEAVIEST CROSS.

" He stood foursquare to every blast,
Tides ebbed and flowed, but he stood fast,
Men found him where they found him last."
Written of D. L. MOODY.

DURING the long fight with the East India
Company, the Mission at Serampore had been
encountering serious internal difficulties. The younger
men who had come out to the work naturally found
irksome the hard discipline to which their predecessors
had subjected themselves. It was one thing willingly
to adopt such an economy, but quite another matter
to find it imposed upon them without choice.

Unacquainted with the extraordinary hardships
undergone by the pioneers, and the violent tempests
through which they had been forced to steer the
Mission, the recruits accepted with poor grace the
authority exercised by Carey, Marshman, and Ward
in the councils of the work. They had strong faith
in their new ideas, and demanded that consideration
be given to them. They claimed that the principle
of equality upon which the conduct of the Mission
had been regulated gave them an equal voice with
their more experienced brethren.

Complaints found their way home, and Fuller, in
the name of the Committee, wrote out to say that

the principle of equality was not to be allowed in the governing committee on the field, but that the Society looked to Carey and his two associates as the men responsible for the disbursement of their funds.

With much regard for the feelings of their colleagues, the triumvirate met this by letting the seven men proceed to out-stations, where they would be virtually self-governing. The rates of allowance were fixed at Rs. 70 per family, of which Rs. 10 was to be considered as for their personal needs and the remainder to be accounted for to the Serampore committee. With this plan Carey expected to see a hundred out-stations set up eventually, but it pre-supposed a devotedness to the cause scarcely to be expected. Carey's gentleness and evident freedom from self-seeking did much to tide over the difficulty, but fresh sources of friction were constantly occurring.

In 1815 Andrew Fuller died, his fine constitution undermined by his heavy labours in the cause of Missions. A man of splendid intellect, extraordinary breadth of judgment, and tender sympathy, he was an administrator of the first order; and the debt that Foreign Missions owes to his unwearying and undaunted efforts is very great. Beloved in his own Church, respected by all, it was nevertheless by the men at the front that he was most intimately understood and appreciated.

To them and their work his loss was irreparable. Sutcliffe had died the previous year, and now with Fuller gone the only link left with the old days was Ryland. Unhappily, with him the silver cord of confidence was already broken, and his attitude grew continually more censorious and unfriendly. For twenty years the lives of the Serampore men were embittered and their energies cramped by the withdrawal of the sympathy of their Committee and by a veritable campaign of misrepresentation.

None of the new members of the Home Committee were personally acquainted with the three leaders at Serampore, and they seem to have acquired from the beginning a distrust of these heroic men. Circumstances had changed of recent years, and ample funds were now at the disposal of the Society, so that it was no longer necessary for the missionaries to be stinted in allowance or forced to earn their own living. Willing, therefore, to send money liberally to the field, the Committee expected in return a spirit of subordination to their views that was strange to the older missionaries. Men who had created so great a work, and who had supported it with unique munificence from their own earnings, could ill brook the immediate change of tone adopted by the Committee, and resented the term of "senior servants of the Society."

At the first meeting of the Committee after Fuller's death, unfriendly hints were thrown out regarding the conduct of the Serampore missionaries, and they were given to understand that investigations were to be made of some of their proceedings, especially with regard to the manner in which they had used funds entrusted to them. Their amazement on finding that they were expected to vindicate their integrity was painful. They were, furthermore, to make immediate arrangements to secure to the Society all buildings at Serampore—largely their own private purchase— while the assistants they had taken on in the field were to be considered as directly under the Home Committee and they themselves but the agents of the Society for the supervision of these.

Such an attitude seemed-calculated to destroy the whole economy of the Mission, and they were filled with consternation and anxiety. Conscious that, so far from making gain of their position, they had spontaneously given tens of thousands of pounds earned by their own toil to the work, it is not to be wondered at if they repelled the insinuation with a measure of indignation.

Ward paid a visit to England, a year or two later, in enfeebled health, under medical orders, and the opportunity was taken of trying to increase the general interest in the Serampore work and of coming to an understanding with the Committee. But to his sorrow he discovered that the gravest imputations regarding the character of himself and his associates had been scattered broadcast, and it had become the general belief that they had amassed colossal fortunes at the expense of the work they went to do. The reputation they had acquired by years of labour had been blasted in a few months.

This cruel cloud of suspicion was a heavy burden to the men of Serampore, but they toiled on in their large sphere without intermission or slackening of effort. Subscriptions came in more and more slowly, and they began to feel the pinch severely. Anxious for the welfare of the work, they drew up another document containing an examination of their affairs, showing exactly what funds they had acquired and received from the very beginning. As we have already seen, £50,000 of their own earning had been devoted entirely to the Mission. Beyond this, £80,000 had been received by them, much of it by their own efforts, and the expenditure of this was shown in detail. The whole was couched in singularly mild language, and should have freed them for ever from suspicion. Unhappily for them, it never saw the light of day, for Dyer, on receipt of it, persuaded his Committee to keep it under lock and key.

For seven years more these unhappy relations continued with increasing tension, and ended in 1827 in an entire separation from the Society. The younger missionaries opened a new centre in Calcutta, taking over with consent several of the Serampore outstations.

Looking back over the controversy, even from this long distance, it is not easy to pass an unbiased judgment. While the Committee naturally pleaded that " the first principle of all missionary societies " demanded submission on the part of the missionaries, they ignored the fact that Serampore had really preceded the missionary societies. The Baptist Missionary Society has long since recognised that a grievous mistake was made, and to-day justly honours the memory of the men who were its first representatives in the foreign field.

Hostile attacks against Serampore continued with unabated force for three years longer, and were at the time deeply injurious to the well-being and support of the work. The strain bore heavily upon the aged men, and in 1830 they gladly brought the long struggle to an end by drawing up a new trust deed. In this they made over the whole of the Serampore properties to eleven trustees in England, some of whom were members of the Baptist Missionary Society.

Throughout the unhappy years their attitude was one of great nobility and Christian fortitude, and this crowning act of self-sacrifice was a conclusion worthy of the disinterested devotion of their whole lives.

CHAPTER XVI.

SERAMPORE COLLEGE.

"We are not offering Salvation by Education for Salvation by Grace. There is no antagonism between what God reveals to us through grace and what He enables us to acquire."—F. JOHNSON.

FROM the beginning Carey had felt that the ultimate method for the evangelisation of India was that of trained native preachers. As the years went by this conviction deepened. He and his fellow-missionaries recognised that their work, far-reaching as it was, was largely preparatory. Theirs it was to plant the gospel flag in every city, to win for Christ a nucleus of men and women, to build up in faith and practice a Church of God in the land, to supply it with the Scriptures in its own tongue, and then to expect that the Spirit of the living God would carry forward the great campaign through these He had saved.

They looked for the uprising of gifted and earnest men who should become apostles to their own people. They had greatly rejoiced in the devoted labours of their converts, but with unerring foresight they kept before them the idea of an institution where such men might receive a broad and efficient education to fit them for the manifold duties of leadership in the Christian Church. This long-cherished hope found its fulfilment in the year 1818, when Serampore College was built.

A site was chosen near the Hooghly, exactly opposite Barrackpore Park, the residence of the Governor-General, and a noble building of Grecian style was erected. It cost the large sum of £15,000, almost the whole of which was raised by the three missionaries, their own private gifts covering no small part of the total cost. The task was undertaken, moreover, at a time when they were almost overwhelmed with other cares, labouring under an eclipsed reputation, and almost forsaken by even their sturdiest friends.

The aim of this unique institution, the first of its kind in the mission field, was plainly avowed to be the equipping of native preachers and evangelists, but the scope of the work was arranged on a generous basis

They felt that a purely theological training might produce too professional and narrow a ministry, and therefore the syllabus of study included Hindu religions, Sanskrit, and Arabic, besides European science and knowledge. A normal school for teachers also was to be conducted under the auspices of the faculty. The institution was to be open to youths from all parts of India without distinction of creed, especial care being taken to make it possible for non-Christian students to enter without compromise.

The scheme was remarkable for its sound general principles, though a mistake was made in subordinating the teaching of English to that of Oriental languages.

The Danish Governor of Serampore and the three missionaries were constituted the trustees, and the annual expense of the college was estimated at £2000. Towards this, Ward, who was then travelling in England and America, succeeded in collecting a considerable sum, though under the greatest difficulties. But more valuable than the money he secured was the assistance of a young man named John Mack, a Scotsman of twenty-three years of age, and a brilliant scholar, who accompanied him on his return to Serampore. Mack was as remarkable for his earnestness and eloquence as for his learning, and he became a most congenial associate for Carey and his coadjutors. Carey was installed as Professor of Divinity, Zoology, and Botany; and Marshman, his son John, and Mack, with a number of moulvies and pundits, provided a

SERAMPORE COLLEGE.

strong staff. The work began with thirty-seven students, of whom eighteen were non-Christians.

Confident of the great future before the institution, Marshman was commissioned, on his visit to England in 1826, to obtain from the Danish king the power to confer degrees and thus to place the undertaking on a satisfactory basis for future development. He was graciously received by the kind sovereign at Copenhagen, who again affirmed his deep interest in the work of the Mission, and, with the consent of the

University, conferred the desired power upon their college. The royal charter, richly bound in vellum at the expense of the Danish Treasury, was sent to Dr. Marshman free of cost.

Launched successfully on its career, the institution started with every prospect of permanent and wide usefulness. The kindliness of the Danish Government was preserved to the last, for when, in 1845, Serampore was sold by Denmark to the East India Company, the treaty expressly provided that the college should retain all the powers granted under the Danish charter. But within a few years of the opening of the college, Calcutta began to take its rightful place as the centre for education, and it gradually became evident that Serampore was not an ideal situation for so large a venture. Degrees were never won, and through the long years of the nineteenth century the institution has had a somewhat precarious existence.

A change has come at last, however, within the last few years. The original large plans for its conduct have been revived, and, once more under a strong faculty, the college has begun a new history. The continued legality of its charter has been acknowledged by the Government of India, and it has the right, unique in all the fields of modern missionary enterprise, of conferring degrees in divinity. This power is at last to be used.

After years of shadow it is coming into its own, and remains to-day the finest monument of the zeal of the early men of Serampore, who planned so wisely and carried their plans to such an extraordinary height of success.

CHAPTER XVII.

CAREY'S HOME LIFE.

"The cheerful old man."—From a *Tribute by Lord Hastings.*

CAREY had seven children, all of whom were born in England except the youngest, and only four of them grew up. Of these, three became missionaries, to the father's great satisfaction.

The youngest, Jonathan, who was born in Mudnabatty, took to the law and practised in Calcutta. William, the second son, laboured quietly in the Mission, chiefly at Dinagepore. Jabez found his field in distant Amboyna, among the Malays, where he was invited to act by the Calcutta Government as State Superintendent of Schools. The many letters addressed to him by his father reveal a depth of affection that is very pleasing, accompanied by a constant anxiety lest the son prove unworthy of the Gospel. The temptations to worldliness that beset Jabez and his wife in their semi-official position were all too potent. He found innumerable obstacles in the way of preaching, and eventually, to his father's sorrow, he formally relinquished his missionary work.

But Felix, the eldest, had the most remarkable experience of any of the family. He, more perhaps than the others, inherited his father's unusual linguistic abilities. A missionary at fifteen, he had studied medicine in Calcutta, and after some service in Serampore he went at the age of twenty-one with a fellow-missionary to Rangoon to found a mission to the Burmese. His companion soon afterwards departed for Colombo, leaving him alone. With such diligence did he apply himself to the language that he was offered the post of interpreter to the Burmese Government. Within a few months he was again at Serampore to print a Burmese grammar and a translation of Matthew that he had prepared. Returning to Rangoon, he found promising opportunities of advancement in the service of the Government, and to his delight was summoned to Ava, the capital, to vaccinate the king's household. A trip to Calcutta to obtain the necessary lymph proved disastrous, for as they came back up the Irrawaddy his boat capsized in a squall and his wife and children were drowned.

He was received graciously by the king, and was made the recipient of a "barbaric title" and other honours. His desire for missionary work became less keen, and he showed much willingness to remain as a dependant of the Burmese monarch, to his father's great distress. "Whenever I think of your relinquishing your post," he wrote, "I shrink back from the idea with a kind of horror, as if I realised it to be a great crime."

Soon afterwards Felix was sent to Calcutta as the representative of the Burmese Court in some negotiations which were then pending. His father was deeply mortified at this, and lamented that, "*Felix is shrivelled from a missionary into an ambassador.*" His mission was unsuccessful, and on his return to Burma he had to fly for his life. Utterly ashamed and disheartened, the young man disappeared among the wild tribes of the Assam Hills and passed through "a succession of adventures that would be considered extraordinary in a novel." After three years of this romantic life, he fell in with Ward at Chittagong, and was induced to return to Serampore. The discipline of trouble had wrought an effectual change in him, and he was enabled to render most valuable assistance in the revision of the Bengali translation before his death, which occurred four years later.

THE COLLEGE HOUSE, SERAMPORE: CAREY'S LAST HOME.

Carey's second marriage was as romantic as his first had been unhappy. There had resided for some time at Serampore in a house of her own, the Lady Rumohr, of a noble family of Schleswig, and sister-in-law of the Chamberlain of the Danish king. She had become well known to the missionaries, having, indeed, been converted in the Mission chapel. She had received a liberal education in her younger days, and was an accomplished linguist. Like so many at that time, she had been driven into infidelity by the lifeless teaching of orthodox Lutheranism; but after her conversion her character was marked by deep piety, and she became a most ardent lover of Missions. During girlhood she had been injured in a fire which rendered her a lifelong sufferer, diminutive in stature and somewhat deformed in appearance; but she won all hearts by her sweetness of disposition, her patrician grace blending with a captivating simplicity.

To this lady Carey was married in the year 1808. She was of the same age as he, both being now in middle life. The years of their union were the happiest that Carey ever knew, for he found in the society of his accomplished wife a depth of fellowship and a wholesome relaxation to which he had hitherto been a stranger. The delicate little lady spent two or three hours a day, morning and evening, in the open air, wheeled about in her tiny carriage as she visited the schools and homes of the people, carrying everywhere the same sunshine with which she brightened the scholar's home.

During his continual absences she wrote him the most tender and courtly letters, many of which, faded and worn, are still preserved.

"MY DEAREST LOVE,—I felt very much in parting from thee," she wrote during a short absence from Serampore, "and feel much in being so far from thee. . . . I am sure thou will be happy and thankful on account of my voice, which is daily growing better, and thy pleasure greatly adds to my own.

"I hope thou will not think I am writing too often; I rather trust thou will be glad to hear from me. . . . Though my journey is very pleasant, and the good state of my health, the freshness of the air, and the rarity of objects enliven my spirits, yet I cannot help longing for you. Pray, my love, take care of your health that I may have the joy to find you well."

Her solicitude for his health and comfort was unceasing, and during the thirteen years of their union they enjoyed the most entire oneness of mind, never having a single circumstance that they concealed one from the other. Her death in 1821 was the severest trial of Carey's life.

Carey's early love of Nature remained with him throughout his life. In his first letter from Calcutta he asked for some botany books to be sent to him, and at Mudnabatty, amid many discouragements, he rejoiced in the care of a well-ordered garden. In a letter to America in 1801 he asks that a Captain Hague be reminded of his promise to get some American productions for the Mission House grounds, and his general correspondence contained many allusions to the solace and pleasure he received from natural history.

As the Mission extended and labourers went far afield he was urgent in his requests for specimens of all kinds to be sent to him. In 1809 he wrote to his son, then a new missionary at Dinagepore: "When you come down take a little pains to bring a few plants of some sort. There is one grows plentifully about Sadamahal as high as one's knee, and produces a red flower. Put half a dozen plants in a pot (with a hole in the bottom). There is at Sadamahal (for I found it there) a plant which produces a flower of a pale bluish colour. . . . Try and bring something. . . . Can't you bring the grasshopper which has a saddle on its back, or the bird with the large crest which he opens when he settles on the ground?"

Again he wrote: "You may always enclose a pinch

of seeds in a letter. Can you not get me," he says, "a khokora, I mean the great bird like a kite, which makes so great a noise, and often carries off a duck or a kid? I believe it is an eagle, and I want to examine it. Send me also all the sorts of ducks and waterfowls you can get, and, in short, every sort of bird you can obtain which is not common here. Collect me all the sorts of insects and serpents and lizards you can get. Put all the insects together in a bottle of rum, except butterflies . . . and serpents and lizards the same. . . . Let me have all the birds alive; and when you have got a boatload send a small boat down with them under charge of a careful person, and I will pay the expenses."

Even as early as 1795 he had said: "I have separate books for every distinct class, as birds, beasts, fishes, reptiles, etc. . . . I am making collections and minute descriptions of whatever I can obtain, and intend at some future time to transmit them to Europe." In a letter to Ryland he says: "We sent you a box some time ago, full of gods and butterflies."

Four years later, however, he has not sent specimens home to any large extent, for fear they should " mock the expectations of our numerous friends, who are waiting to hear of the conversion of the heathen and the weakening of Satan's kingdom." Many of the objects collected by him are to be seen to-day at Serampore College, along with the chair he used, his grammars and translations, and many other objects of interest.

On settling at Serampore two acres of land, afterwards increased to five, were set apart for his garden. Carefully walled in so that the villagers' cattle and dogs might not intrude, he collected here specimens of all that was choice and rare in tropical flowers and trees, and attempted also to grow the products of other climes. The first potatoes ever grown in Bengal were planted by him; and his grapes were so fine as to be thought worthy of presentation to the Governor-General himself. Mahogany trees that he planted attracted, till quite recently, the notice of visitors. Such European flowers and shrubs as would live in the damp, hot atmosphere, he carefully tended, and a large band of native gardeners was kept constantly at work.

He rejoiced to have around him the flowers of his native land, for the love of home was strong in his heart though he never came home, and in writing to a kind friend he tells of an unexpected pleasure in this connection. "That I might be sure not to lose any part of your valuable present, I shook the bag over a patch of earth in a shady place; on visiting which, a few days afterwards, I found springing up, to my inexpressible delight, a *bellis perennis* of our English pastures. I know not that I ever enjoyed, since leaving Europe, a simple pleasure so exquisite as the sight this English daisy afforded me, not having seen one for thirty years, and never expecting to see one again."

His beautiful garden was largely destroyed in the flood of 1823, though he afterwards re-made it as lovely as ever. Eight years later a cyclone uprooted many of his trees, and the sight of the desolation brought the old man to tears.

One day, during his last illness, when he appeared unusually depressed, Dr. Marshman asked him the cause. "Ah," he ruefully replied, looking away, "I was thinking that when I die Brother Marshman will let the cows into my garden."

CHAPTER XVIII.

CAREY'S PARISH.

"The restless millions wait
That light whose coming maketh all things new,
God also waits, but men are slow and late."

THE spirit that stirred John Wesley when he exclaimed, "The world is my parish," was the spirit that possessed Carey from the time when he manufactured his globe out of the remnants of his shoemaking, and pasted the large map of the world on the wall of his village workshop.

We have already had evidence of this in the appeal he sent home from the Indian Ocean, and the desire expressed on his removal to Mudnabatty that his allowance be used for a missionary to another land. And it was his constant habit of thought to dwell upon the needs of the lands which sat in darkness with no one to carry them the light. In his praying, as in his thinking, he claimed them all for Christ, and watched with eagerness for open doors through which the gospel might enter.

Soon after landing in India he wrote home : "I have been mentioned by a person high in office, and utterly unknown to, and unthought of by, me, as a proper person to send to Tibet and Assam, to make discoveries that they have much at heart. Should this take place, it would open a new and wide door for usefulness in a

INSIDE CAREY'S CHURCH : THE BAPTISTERY.

country remote from the knowledge of Europeans."
He welcomes the idea, "but," he adds, "these nations
are afraid that the English have designs to subjugate
them as they have Bengal!"

Every event was read by him in terms of evangelisation. In 1804 he says: "The Maratha war and the
subjugation of the country of Cuttak to the English
may be esteemed a favourable event for the spreading
of the gospel." Burma seemed to be constantly
beckoning to him. Ever accurate in his knowledge,
apostolic in outlook, and youthfully enthusiastic in
his keenness for advance, he wrote to Fuller in 1806:
"The Burman Empire is 800 miles long, lying con-
tiguous to Bengal on the east; but it is inaccessible
by land on account of the mountains covered with
thick forests which run between the two countries.
The eastern side of the Empire borders on China,
Cochin-China, and Tonking, and may afford us an
opportunity ultimately of introducing the gospel
into those countries. *They are quite within our reach,*
and the Bible in Chinese will be understood by them
as well as by the Chinese themselves."

In 1809, after having enjoyed almost unbroken
health for many years past, "not having leisure to
be ill," he was seized with a fever which brought him
so low that for some days his life was despaired of.
His desires dwelt so much upon the extension of
Christ's kingdom that even when his mind was
wandering he was filled with this one idea. He
fancied in his delirium he had received a commission
from God to go forth to every land, to all princes
and governments, to require them to abolish all
political establishments of religion, and to declare
war infamous and intolerable. Angels attended him,

and princes who were refractory were struck dead by heavenly attendants.

In a letter telling of his recovery he reminded them at home of the long centuries that had elapsed since the gospel was first given for all men, and of the little progress made. " Hindostan," he wrote, " requires ten thousand ministers of the gospel." Happy would he have been could he have known that a hundred years

CAREY'S CHURCH (EXTERIOR).

later that land would have more than five thousand missionaries labouring within its borders, assisted by an army of 35,000 Indian workers!

He went on to take a review of the state of Asia, and urged the necessity of missions to Siam, Pegu, Aracan, Nepaul, Assam, and all the other countries lying on the borders of the British dominions. He pleads for consideration to be given to places still farther afield, enumerating as among the most urgent,

China, Sumatra, Java, Cambodia, the Moluccas, and the Philippines, Africa, and South America.

Nor does this seem wildly extravagant when we realise the remarkable manner in which his own work was spreading. In 1810 he could tell of five distinct fields, all sprung from Serampore : Bengal, Bhutan, Burma, Orissa, and Hindustan (Upper India). Before long Surat in the west and Nagpur in the centre of India were occupied, and then, as if these responsibilities were not sufficient, further work was started in places so diverse as Java, Amboyna, Penang, Ceylon, and Mauritius. Members of their Church, Anglo-Indians apparently, and engaged in trade, had fared forth as far as Bourbon, Isle of France, and Madagascar, and they carried the influence of Serampore to those distant places. A Pushto version of the Scriptures had been prepared and sent up to the great North-west, and Carey was sanguine of shortly following it up with missionaries to the Panjab, Kashmir, and even Afghanistan.

Financial assistance sent to Bengal by America was repaid later when in 1812 the first American missionaries, Judson and Newell, sought an asylum at Serampore, whence Judson eventually reached Burma to inaugurate the mighty movement in that land. Work had been started there by Serampore emissaries, but with that splendid disinterestedness that springs out of the deepest interest in the people Carey and his fellows did not hesitate to encourage to the utmost of their powers the new venture.

"Our attempts in the Burmese Empire," he wrote to the American Board, "have ended in the transfer of the Mission to Brother Judson, and those whom you have sent to join him. Something, however, has been done: a Mission House has been built; the language has been opened; a grammar printed; materials for a dictionary found; a portion of the New Testament published, and copies of it circulated." They even presented Judson with a printing press and type.

In Britain, meanwhile, there was much to enocurage those who cared for the evangelisation of the world. "The spark which God stirred you up to strike," wrote Fuller, just before his death, "has kindled a great fire." Missionary societies were springing up in every denomination, both in England and Scotland. To Carey this was a matter of intense satisfaction. "I rejoice much at the missionary spirit; surely it is a prelude to the universal spread of the gospel!"

Carey's vision was so far imparted to the nation that even Parliament was forced to accept the verdict of Serampore on their policy in subject lands; and the revived glow of apostolic enthusiasm that began at the first to be felt in the district of Olney became the abiding possession of the Anglo-Saxon race.

CHAPTER XIX.

THE SECRETS OF SUCCESS.

"My heart is wedded to India."—CAREY at 65.

CAREY'S life is a record of the transforming power of Divine grace. Of peasant birth, without the early benefits of cultured home or association, and spending many of his years in grinding poverty, he grew withal into a splendid type of a Christian gentleman.

His own recognition of what Christian manhood implied is best appreciated from a letter written to his son Jabez on the occasion of his setting out for Amboyna. "Behave affably and genteely to all," he says, "but not cringing towards any. Feel that you are a man, and always act with that dignified sincerity and truth which will command the esteem of all. Seek not the society of worldly men, but when called to be with them, act and converse with propriety and dignity. To do this, labour to get a good acquaintance with men and things. A gentleman is the next best character after a Christian, and the latter includes the former. Money never makes a gentleman, neither does a fine appearance, but an enlarged understanding joined to engaging manners."

His fine courtesy was seen to advantage in those early years in India when, without the support of congenial associates, he bore the upbraidings of his insane wife and the follies of Thomas with never a word of reproach for either. His peasant origin showed itself in a certain shyness through life, which, however, only added to the charm of his personality. Even when, by his patient industry and the example of a noble and self-sacrificing life, he had won the esteem and friendship of men in the highest social circles, he evinced no desire to disclaim his lowly birth.

CAREY'S COMMUNION SERVICE.

"Was not Dr. Carey once a shoemaker?" said a General in scorn to his aide-de-camp, when he had just met the venerable missionary at a social gathering. "No, sir," said Dr. Carey, quietly turning on the questioner, "only a cobbler."

It was this very simplicity and the readiness to accept whatever the Master assigned to him that gave him power in all his associations. His colleagues at Serampore loved and revered him with a rare intensity. His intercourse with young missionaries who resented authority, with chaplains and government officials, with scholars and merchants alike, was that of a saint and a gentleman. Gentle, considerate, and free from personal ambition, he always endeavoured to see the best side of every man. His estimate of himself was low. He constantly bewailed his coldness of heart and inability to give himself utterly to his work. " Marshman," he would say, " in point of zeal, is Luther, I am Erasmus ; Ward has a remarkable power of addressing the heart, I can only get out dry sentences. I alone am unfit to be a missionary. I wonder that God tolerates me." In 1823, after another serious illness, he wrote : " I had no fear of death, nor reluctance to die ; but never was I so seriously convinced of the value of an ATONING Saviour as then."

The simplicity of his life was marked, and the scheme of Moravian community life that he advocated was his highest ideal in this respect. He began life exceedingly poor, and remained voluntarily poor throughout. During his whole career he only accepted £600 for himself and his family from the Society he had called into being, while he spent on the evangelisation and civilisation of his adopted land more than £46,000. Pressed to answer charges of self-aggrandisement, he modestly replies, " I am poor, and I can scarcely lay by a sum monthly to relieve three or four indigent relatives in Europe." Words written of Robert Hall, Carey's contemporary in England, might be equally applied to him : " A man who unites with the most profound and varied attainments the fervour of an evangelist, the piety of a saint, and the simplicity of a child."

Uninfluenced by prosperity or adversity, of both of which he had a large share, or by the blandishments of admirers, he retained his early devotion to his work undimmed through the long years. " Though we have much business upon our Hands . . . our Hearts have not been taken from our grand Object," was his testimony. With the solitary exception of his gardening, he seems never to have allowed himself any respite from his labours. Recreation he found in change of employment.

The spirit of the work is revealed in a quaint letter of Ward's, regarding the resignation of a young missionary who had shown no aptitude for the hard service: "In our work half the dissenting ministers in England, who merely preach twice or thrice a week, when people come to hear, would be of little use. A man who shall do good here must be incessantly on his legs, or in the saddle, or in his boat. In the hands of a mere domesticated man, who stays at home and never goes out into the highways and ditches, things die a natural death."

The Serampore missionaries, assuredly, were no mere domesticated men! Toiling with might and main, their sole aim was to enthrone Christ.

CHAPTER XX.

THE BORDERLAND.

"Thou'rt in our heart—with tresses thin and grey,
And eye that knew the Book of Life so well,
And brow serene, as thou wert wont to stray
Amidst thy flowers—like Adam ere he fell."
Lines by a CONTEMPORARY.

CAREY'S constitution had been sturdy, but the stress of three decades of service in India had sapped much of his early strength, and now occasional attacks of illness made life more difficult for him. And he was lonely. It was a blessing to him therefore when, in 1822, he married Mrs. Hughes, a widow of forty-five. She possessed none of the accomplishments of the Lady Rumohr, but she was a woman of sound Christian character, and a more tender and kindly companion Carey could not have had during his remaining years.

A few months after his marriage, as he was returning from Calcutta at midnight, his foot slipped as he stepped on shore and the hip-joint was severely injured. The agony was intense for several days, and his friends scarcely expected that he would recover. But once again, in the mercy of God, he was brought back to his loved work.

While he was still confined to his bed a terrible flood occurred on the Hooghly, and, owing to the bursting of an embankment, the town of Serampore was inundated. The river bank in front of Carey's

house was swept away, and the roaring torrent
approached nearer and nearer until it was rolling past
within ten feet of the sufferer. Not till then would
he allow his bed to be carried away to another building,
and he was removed only just in time, for the house
disappeared shortly afterwards.

A sudden and almost overwhelming blow occurred
later in the same year. Ward, the beloved colleague,
died from cholera. The three men had lived and
laboured together for twenty-three years as if animated
by one soul, and the survivors seemed unable for a
time to recover from the shock. To add to their
burden, heavy financial embarrassments quickly succeeded each other.

The flood had done a great deal of damage to the
Mission premises and brought fresh and severe expenses
upon the missionaries, while the constant needs of their
large work were inadequately met by funds from
England. Practically nothing came to them from the
Society, and others hesitated to give until confidence
was restored in the probity of the overburdened
missionaries.

Counting upon a magnificent promise of £13,000
from England for Bible translation, work was carried
forward with increased eagerness, though it involved
borrowing at heavy interest in Calcutta. By an unfortunate re-arrangement of the method of disbursing
the huge sum raised in England, the missionaries at
Serampore found themselves debarred from it, and the
whole expense fell back upon them. They had just
spent £15,000 on the college, and now a debt of
£10,000 hung, as they expressed it, like a millstone
around their necks. When their great difficulty
became known, however, to the British and Foreign

Bible Society, a magnanimous gift of money was sent to them, by the help of which they succeeded in clearing off the whole debt.

It was at this time that, owing to the expense of the Burmese War, the Government determined to give up Fort William College. This was an utterly unexpected blow, for Carey's salary was at once reduced to a pension of Rs. 500 a month. By the abolition of the Bengali translatorship, a post Carey had accepted in order to raise more money for the work, a further £300 a year ceased to come in.

The missionaries met for special prayer, for the emergency was the most serious they had yet faced. "The two old men were dissolved in tears while they engaged in prayer," wrote one who was present, "and Dr. Marshman especially could not give expression to his feelings. It was indeed affecting to see these good men—the fathers of the Mission—entreating with tears that God would not forsake them now grey hairs were come upon them, but that He would silence the voice of calumny and furnish them with the means of carrying on His own work."

Rising from their knees, they drew up an appeal for help, which they sent home to the Baptist Missionary Society, from which they were now separated, and to the general Christian public of Britain. "If," they wrote, "increasing industry and self-denial could by any means furnish us with the supplies we beg of you, we would toil and deny ourselves with cheerful alacrity."

And once more their needs were met, for money soon came in from England sufficient for all their present necessities. The appeal seemed to restore confidence in them at last. The relief was most seasonable, and the work took upon it a spirit of animation and zeal that had never been exceeded in the earlier days. New ardour and hopefulness appeared in all departments, and the missionaries began to think that they had at length come into quiet waters.

Their hopes, alas, were doomed to disappointment. With the beginning of 1833 there came upon Calcutta the most serious financial crisis it had ever experienced. A series of great commercial disasters followed one another in rapid succession. The chief mercantile houses of the Indian metropolis were shaken to their foundations, and many failed.

Upon the Serampore missionaries the blow fell heavily. Funds devoted to special purposes had been lodged with firms that failed, and all were swept away. Carey lost all he had set aside for his family, and Marshman was in a similar case.

Again they were forced to appeal to England. "Our wants for the stations are not great," they pleaded, "for they do not exceed £2000 a year; and when sixteen mission stations, with forty-seven labourers, can have their wants supplied for such a sum, we know not how missionary operations can be conducted with greater economy." When the state of affairs became known in England, friends once more rallied to the help of the men at the front, and the great work was saved from destitution.

It was the last fight for Carey. He was now seventy-two years of age, and his race was nearly run. "His last days," says Dr. Smith, "were the best. His sun went down in all the splendour of a glowing faith and a burning self-sacrifice."

His faithful colleague, Marshman, has given us a

description of him in those later days : " Though thus
reduced in circumstances, the good man is as cheerful
and as happy as the day is long. He rides out four or
five miles every morning, returning home by sunrise;
goes on with the work of translation day by day;
gives two lectures on divinity and one on natural
history every week in the college, and takes his turn at
preaching."

" A little yellow old man," Duff describes him, " in a
white jacket, who tottered up to the visitor of whom
he had already often heard, and with outstretched arms
solemnly blessed him."

Another pleasing picture of him is supplied by Gogerly
of the London Mission, who saw him in his last year :
" He was seated near his desk, in the study, dressed in
his usual neat attire; his eyes were closed, and his
hands clasped together. . . . His appearance as he sat
there, with the few white locks that adorned his venerable brow, and his placid colourless face, filled me with
a kind of awe; for he appeared as then listening for
the Master's summons, and as waiting to depart."

He was busy to the end, busy with the work he
loved; and when he completed his last revision of the
Bengali translation, he felt, like the Venerable Bede,
that his work was accomplished. His garden was still
his earthly paradise. Until quite unable to leave his
bed he delighted to be drawn in a chair down the
paths beneath the wide-spreading trees and amid the
shrubs and creepers that blossomed opulently with
purple and scarlet. And so he ended where he began
—among his flowers and with his books. The same
pleasures were enjoyed by the old man as those that
gladdened the boy, with the addition that the old man
had GOD; the God he had first come to know in the

cobbler's shop, the same God who had been with him
all the long way of life, only greater and more wonderful now than ever before.

Duff, on one of the last visits he paid to the aged

CAREY'S GRAVE AT SERAMPORE, AND THE TOMB OF HIS WIFE.

scholar, was leaving after a season of prayer and
converse.   He heard his name feebly called, and turned
back.   " Mr. Duff," came the whisper, " you have been
speaking about Dr. Carey, Dr. Carey ; when I am gone
say nothing about Dr. Carey—speak about Dr. Carey's
Saviour."

Death he waited for peacefully and with perfect resignation. "Respecting the great change before him," wrote Mack, "not a single shade of anxiety has crossed his mind since the beginning of his decay, so far as I am aware. His Christian experience partakes of that *guileless integrity* which has been the grand characteristic of his life He is ripe for glory." " I have no fears, I have no doubts, I have not a wish left unsatisfied," he said to Marshman a few days before his death.

On Monday morning, 9th June 1834, he quietly passed away, in the presence of those he loved most. The following morning he was buried in the Mission burial ground. Men and women of all classes followed him to the grave, while the route was lined with Hindus and Mohammedans who desired to show their last respects for one so universally loved. The flag at Barrackpore, over the river, flew at half-mast as when some royal person has died.

In the little cemetery the tomb is still to be seen. Approaching the gate by a narrow lane, the visitor finds it just within, on the left—a block of masonry surmounted by a domed canopy resting on four pillars. It bears the simple inscription chosen by Carey himself—

WILLIAM CAREY
BORN AUGUST 17, 1761.
DIED JUNE 9, 1834.

———

"A wretched, poor and helpless worm,
On Thy kind arms I fall."

6·99